About *The Believer* magazine

The Believer is a magazine offering essays, interviews, reviews, and advice, the latter of which appears in the form of a monthly column called "Sedaratives." The Sedaratives column, which started in May 2005 with advice by Amy Sedaris, gave rise to this book.

About the Editor

Eric Spitznagel is a contributing editor for *The Believer* magazine, where he cocreated (along with Amy Sedaris) the Sedaratives column. He's also the author of six books and a frequent contributor to *Playboy* and *Vanity Fair*. He has one more testicle than Hitler, which he considers a moral victory.

You're a Horrible Person, But I Like You

THE BELIEVER BOOK OF ADVICE

You're a Horrible Person, But I Like You

THE BELIEVER BOOK OF ADVICE

With Sarah Silverman, Zach Galifianakis,
Fred Armisen, Judd Apatow, & many more

INTRODUCTION BY DAVID CROSS

Edited by Eric Spitznagel

VINTAGE BOOKS

A Division of Random House, Inc.

New York

Library of Congress Cataloging-in-Publication Data
You're a horrible person, but I like you : the Believer book of advice / with Sarah Silverman, Zach Galifianakis, Fred Armisen, Judd Apatow, & many more ; introduction by David Cross, edited by Eric Spitznagel.
p. cm.
ISBN: 978-0-307-47523-7
1. American wit and humor.   2. Advice columns—Humor.
I. The Believer magazine.
PN6165.Y68 2010
814'.54—dc22
2010001857

Book design by Debbie Glasserman

www.vintagebooks.com

Printed in the United States of America
10 9 8 7 6 5 4 3 2 1

Contents

You're a Horrible Person, But I Like You

THE BELIEVER BOOK OF ADVICE

Introduction

Dear David Cross:

We're thinking about publishing a book of advice. It would involve getting a bunch of our favorite comedians and writers and actors (and whoever else is available) to answer questions on a variety of topics, particularly those in which they have very little knowledge or experience. Does this seem like a good idea?

Best,
The Believer *magazine*
San Francisco, CA

Dear *The Believer* magazine:
Unfortunately, I cannot answer your impertinent question with a simple "Sure" or "Ha-ha! Wait, you're not serious, are you?" answer. I'm afraid this will take a great deal of thought and therefore time. I'm not sure that I have that time to give. I am currently in the middle of *Doodle City: Legend of Kylarath*,

and I am very close to getting an upgrade for my Shield of the Ancients and the magic grapes from the Innkeeper. I don't know that I can or want to help you. But . . . a deal is a deal, yes?

What you have done for me is unforgivable. Sorry, Freudian slip. Un*forgettable* is what I meant. Okay then, let's do this. I will need to take off the next three weeks from work. (I am a life coach for Jack Welch.) Given that, I am booking a flight now to Upper Mongolia, where I can meditate on the answer unmolested by technology or beauty.

There. I have booked it. Computers!!

The flight leaves tonight from Newark. It is costly and I am sitting in the back row just across from the toilet. I have been told to bring my own snacks, as none will be provided. I booked it on Orbitz.com less than five minutes ago and have already received four spam e-mails from them. No, I do not want to save up to 35 percent on a flight/hotel package to Disney World.

Before I leave for the airport, let me just ask this: Why? Is this book really necessary? Will it help? Or will it hurt? I mean *really* hurt, like ten waterboardings and an Indian burn on your penis and/or vulva? Have you given that any thought? What about animals? Are they being considered? Especially cute otters? What about the people of Southeast Asia? And why now? How come not in a couple of weeks? I don't understand. I especially don't understand why I am going on this long, involved, inconvenient trip. I could've just taken a bath. Oh well, the ticket has been paid for and is waiting in webspace. If nothing else, I should lose a couple of pounds from the dysentery.

I'm going to take a quick nap and poo before the flight. Later, skater!

(A short while later.)

Well, I am now at the gate and there has been a slight delay due to a military coup that took place earlier this evening in one of the cities we were supposed to stop in on the way. It was in the fictional town of Khurgiztisk. Hashna Hoti was thrown out of office and replaced by his brother Adnan, a high-ranking wizard in World of Warcraft. I am quickly losing power in my iPod as well. But that's okay; I brought along some mix tapes. I'm going to give them to the pilot to stick in the stereo once we level off and attain our cruising altitude. It's mostly Bikini Kill and early Faust. Oh, hang on.

(An indeterminate number of days later.)

Great! The coup failed and we are cleared for takeoff. Adnan Hoti was killed in the public square by children and wolves. Thank the gods! I can now eat those salt-and-vinegar pork rinds I found. The new leader is Grzk Usbghg, a donkey groomer from the early 1900s.

(One flight later.)

I am now back in America and feel well rested if nothing else. You had asked me something earlier before I left the country. What was it? Something about your doing a book of "advice"? Well, before I can answer you, I need to ask a few questions.

1. Will this be a "for-profit" book, or will all monies collected be sent to charity, specifically the International Association for Blinds and Deafs?

2. Will it be "funny"? And if so, will it be smugly absurd or absurdly smug?

3. Who played shortstop for the Atlanta Braves after Rafael Ramírez?

4. Will this be the kind of book I can find and purchase at the airport or will I have to go to a scary anarchist's underground bunker to find it?

5. Will I receive credit toward junior college for this?

6. I believe that five questions are enough. But not more than enough. That would be six questions.

7. Please see question number 6.

Until I receive a satisfactory reply to the above, I'm afraid I can't help you.

> Anxiously awaiting your reply (not really),
> David Cross

Aziz Ansari

Dear Aziz:
My best friend recently asked if my wife is a beard. I don't understand
the question. Is he luring me into a game of absurdist improv? Should
I respond with "No, she's a teapot. Is your wife a Persian rug?"
> *R. Hayes*
> *Bakersfield, CA*

Dear R. Hayes:
Your playful back-and-forth makes it very clear. You should
respond with "Brian, I love you and I want to leave my wife."
Hide your true feelings no more.
> Aziz

...

Dear Aziz:

I just saw my grandma's tattoos. Suddenly I don't want tattoos any-more. (That was the saddest-looking unicorn I've ever seen.) Is there a way of getting rid of a tramp stamp without expensive surgery?

> *Mikayla*
> *Mississauga, ON, Canada*

Dear Mikayla:

Unfortunately, there is no easy way out. The best thing to do is to get tattoos that age well. Perhaps a tattoo of a young Michael Caine, which will age gracefully into a tattoo of an older Michael Caine. Another option is to get a huge arrow tattooed on your back. Have it point to the tat, and at the top write, "I really regret this and I promise I'm not a whore."

> Aziz

...

Dear Aziz:

How long can you spend masturbating to pictures of ex-girlfriends on Facebook before it becomes a problem?

> *Ethan*
> *Boise, ID*

Dear Ethan:

At the current time, I'd say you don't have a problem. But if it moves from Facebook to Twitter and you are simply mas-turbating to her Twitter updates, then it's time to step away and reassess the situation.

> Aziz

...

Dear Aziz:
How does one go about becoming a ward of the state? It sounds like a sweet deal.

> Daniel Wyatt
> Minneapolis, MN

Dear Daniel:
Unfortunately, I'm too lazy to go to Wikipedia or Google and find out exactly what a ward of the state is. The person sitting next to me didn't know either. I suggest you drop this dream.

> Aziz

. . .

Dear Aziz:
Every time I think of her, I get so dizzy that I want to throw up. Am I in love?

> Just Gavin
> Cleveland, OH

Dear Gavin:
This happened to me once, too. You used old milk in the macaroni you just made. Don't eat any more!

> Aziz

. . .

Dear Aziz:
Can a single woman and a married man be "just friends"? We've made jokes like "What's a handjob between pals?" But I'm pretty sure he was just kidding. Oh crap, does he think he's getting a handjob? Dammit!

> Charlotte
> Boston, MA

Dear Charlotte:

I was once a maid in a very posh hotel, and a guest who was running for senator came into the room of a socialite to say hello. I was inside cleaning and was trying on a fancy jacket owned by the socialite. The senatorial candidate walked in and, believing that I was the socialite, went with me on a walk in the park. There was a bond formed based on a lie, but I had to pursue it.

So my answer is I'm not sure; I just wanted to tell someone I was the inspiration for the hit film *Maid in Manhattan*, starring Jennifer Lopez and Ralph Fiennes.

Aziz

Judd Apatow

Dear Judd:
I was talking on the phone with my brother not long ago, and while
we were saying our goodbye I told him I loved him. He seemed hesi-
tant to return the words. I haven't said it again since, but it's been
on my mind. What's wrong with telling your brother you love him?
Could it be some deep-seated homophobia?

Feeling Unloved in Alaska

Dear Feeling Unloved in Alaska:
I am confused. Are these questions for real or is this column a
joke? If this is real, I would say that it is often hard for siblings
to connect after so many difficult years of rivalry and competi-
tion for the love of their parents. If this is a fake letter then I
am not sure what to say. Am I supposed to make a joke?

Judd

...

Dear Judd:
My neighbor's dog has been leaving "surprises" on my front lawn.
I've complained about it repeatedly, but he refuses to curb his dog or,
at the very least, keep the mutt on a leash. Legally, does this give me
the right to take a dump on his property?

> *Ready to Poop*
> *Clearwater, FL*

Dear Ready to Poop:
This one feels like a fake letter. The question is not very
funny or unique. I thought *The Believer* was written by
smart, literate people. Or maybe they are so smart that they
don't know how to write dirty questions and jokes. I wonder
if these questions are lame as some sort of ironic comment on
how the magazine feels about me.

> Judd

...

Dear Judd:
My son was just diagnosed with a wheat allergy. Does this mean
he's going to be rotten at competitive sports?

> *Hand-wringing Father in*
> *St. Louis*

Dear Hand-wringing Father in St. Louis:
Now, this is the type of question that only an egghead
unfunny human can write. When looked at from every possible direction it is devoid of humor. It is also so unfunny
that there's no way for me to spin it funny, even if I comment
on how unfunny it is. I don't see how any of this promotes
Funny People. Maybe that is the whole point. They are so
against that type of promotion and publicity that they invite

me to answer these questions, knowing I will fail. My failure is their intellectual way of attacking me for being commercial. I can't believe *The Believer* is so mean and judgmental.

Judd

...

Dear Judd:
I'm reading a book and I really hate it, but I'm almost done. I think I'm going to finish it, but I'm having an existential crisis re: wasting my life reading a book I hate. On the other hand, my parents raised me to believe that once you read the first page, you're committed to the last page. But this book is just so bad. Any advice?
Claire
Baltimore, MD

Dear Claire:
See, this one feels real. I like this question. I personally own thousands of books and have read maybe twenty in the last five years. I have read one or two pages of all of them. So I say, put it down with pride. Shit, *The Believer* just got me to admit how illiterate and uneducated I am.

Judd

...

Dear Judd:
I'm getting married next weekend and my bride-to-be has decided that we should write our own vows. Can you help me come up with something that's (a) totally romantic, and (b) lets my bros know that I think this is just as queer as they do?
Thanks.
Hoping Not to Look Like a Fag at the Altar
Boston, MA

Dear Hoping Not to Look Like a Fag at the Altar:
This one is clearly a joke meant to comment on the current trend of "bromance comedies," which some have blamed on me. If I answer this one, I am accepting the fact that they think I would use words like "bros" and "queer." So I refuse to respond, even with a joke as a form of protest. Think about my movies, really think about them, and you will see there are all sorts of levels and shit in there.

Judd

...

Dear Judd:
How do I get rid of this cowlick? Besides a hat, I mean.
Confused in San Francisco

Dear Confused in San Francisco:
Now I am embarrassed. I have clearly used an ironic approach to answer these questions as a way to seem like I fit into the style of *The Believer*, when the truth is that I don't even understand what the style of *The Believer* is and actually have a hard time reading it because it's so damn smart. I like twenty-page articles on the history of the Helvetica font and interviews with Todd Haynes as much as the next guy, but I'd be lying if I didn't admit that I like saying I read *The Believer* more than I like actually reading it. It looks great in the magazine rack in my bathroom and sitting on the floor of my office. And even though I have never read one cover-to-cover, I glow in the pride of being a buyer of it when people notice I have it on an airplane or when I read it in front of them so they know I am smart. So fuck you, *The Believer*, for exposing me like this. I don't need you. I think leaving a *McSweeney's* around makes me look cool enough.

Judd

Fred Armisen

Dear Fred:
What do you think is the best way to tell my dad I'm a lesbian? I'm thinking he's already suspicious since I'm thirty-one and haven't yet brought a guy home.

Jennifer Alfonso
Tampa, FL

Dear Jennifer:
I'll tell him. What's his number? Let me practice what I'm going to say to him. "Hi, Mr. Alfonso? I'm Fred Armisen from *Saturday Night Live* on NBC." No, no, no. "Hey! Señor Alfonso! Whatchoo' doin'? Slap me five!" No. "Mr. Alfonso, this is an amazing, weird planet we live on. Look at that sky. Is there a name for such a beautiful color? Let's talk about your daughter." No. I'll figure it out. But again, his number, please.

Fred

...

Dear Fred:
Which is better for cannabis, the cookie or the brownie? Or are we all off track? Should we explore other options, like marmalade or trail mix? Plus, do you have any recipes?

Jack Foster
Queens, NY

Dear Jack:
Leave sweets alone. They don't need your cannabis. Why would you want to ruin a delicious brownie? Here's a recipe: Go out your front door. Get in your car. Drive down the street. Go to a parking lot. Get out of your car and sit on the hood. Think about your question. Think about the fact that you don't know me well enough to ask me a question like that. It's called manners. Have them.

Fred

...

Dear Fred:
I'm a college student turning twenty. The last girlfriend I had was in high school, and that was after three years of asking her out every summer. In college, I find it hard to meet girls with similar interests, like television on DVD or sixty trips to the movie theater a year. Do I have to give up my obviously unsuccessful lifestyle and become more intrepid to find available women, or is there a woman out there sedate enough for me to date?

Na Jo
Chicago, IL

Dear Na:
There are many holes in your story. The numbers don't check out. You're turning twenty but you spent three summers without a girlfriend but you had one in high school? The math doesn't work. Sixty trips to the movie theater a year but you're a full-time student, which means you can only work part-time but you're also into DVDs? It doesn't make sense. What are you really trying to ask me? I know. You want to ask me why my arms are so built. Na! Don't be so shy. Go ahead and ask. It comes from rigorous weight lifting and weight training. Some push-ups, but mostly weights.

Fred

. . .

Dear Fred:
I recently received an e-mail from a female friend whom I'd been romantically involved with over the summer. Things ended badly, and the e-mail was an apology for her jealous behavior. Should I accept her apology?

Andrew McIntyre
Washington, DC

Dear Andrew:
Here's a quote from a speech by Mahatma Gandhi, 1945: "Breakups are hard. Breakups are hard. You say these things and it's like . . . I don't know. I don't get jealous, you know? I just get mad sometimes. Like 'What did that guy say to you?' That kind of thing. A friend of mine is going through this and it's like . . . I know what you're going through. Really."

Hope it helps.

Fred

...

Dear Fred:

When she saw me attempting to clean my ears with a Q-tip, my mother would chide me and say, "The only thing you should put in your ear is your elbow." What is the proper way to clean one's ears and how often should they be cleaned?

Ben Brown
Marietta, GA

Dear Ben:

There's a chemical solution that I like to use. I buy it online. It's a boric protein mixed with dubnium (I think the chemical compound is Db2?) that I insert as a powder before I go to bed. After it settles into my ear canal, I wait an hour and add two drops of calcite (you can get calcite drops at drugstores in Brooklyn and Oakland) that immediately create a loud froth. I then go to my sink and spit out the waxy, bloody remnants. I know it's a little involved, but it does create a thoroughly clean ear.

Fred

...

Dear Fred:

Are there any meats not worth boiling?

Chris Elzinga
San Francisco, CA

Dear Chris:

Do not boil meats! Wow, Chris! What are you doing? Use your grill. Use a pan. Are you from a third-world country? If you are, here's a message to all your countrymen: Don't boil meats! It's one of the main reasons tourists don't visit your third-world country. We get grossed out when we see a pot of boiling water with meats rolling around in it.

Fred

. . .

Dear Fred:

A couple of days after being washed, my hair forms a sort of natural gel that holds any style I desire. Many people have told me that this is disgusting and I should just wash my hair and purchase a commercial hair product. Is it wrong that I choose to save money and go with the styling gel that God gave me?

Mark Iosifescu
New York, NY

Dear Mark:

The people who tell you this are not your friends. You are a punk. Remember that. They don't even know what punk is. They think it's the Police but they are wrong. You know what they are? Preppies. Tell them to go buy another alligator shirt.

Fred

. . .

Dear Fred:

I just got out of rehab and I'm wondering how to get back into the swing of "normal" life. Do you have any pearls of wisdom on how to feel at ease in society without the handy dandy use of any narcotic?

Lorelei Leslie
Santa Monica, CA

Dear Lorelei:

The healthiest thing to do would be to replace your addiction with another (gambling, alcohol, rage, etc.). I went to an addictions specialist and she told me the opposite, but let's ignore that advice. Also, don't forget that it's perfectly fine to lie to yourself about whether or not you're using narcotics.

Fred

...

Dear Fred:

How is it that the mangoes I buy in a jar are so uniform? Is it done by a machine? Who cuts them? When I purchase the jarred and perfectly luscious slices, am I supporting some horrible sweatshop full of miserable mango fabricators, hunched over with fingers puckered and slippery with the mangoes' sweet nectar?

Susan Shuemake
Dallas, TX

Dear Susan:

I forwarded your letter to a mango jarrery in California. This is from the employees:

Dear Susan:

We are writing to you from a horrible sweatshop. It is very sweaty in here. We are mango fabricators and are miserable because it is full of us here. We are hunched over with fingers puckered and slippery with the mangoes' sweet nectar. Please visit us. You can come in on our breaks. 10:15 to 10:30 a.m. is the first one, so do that one.

You should do it, Susan!

Fred

Maria Bamford

Dear Maria:
My little sister is engaged to a total slimeball. I haven't told her
how I feel, because she already thinks I want to sleep with him (long
story). How can I sabotage their relationship without making my
sister hate me forever?

Reluctant Bridesmaid
Glendale, CA

Dear RB in GC:
Slimeballs are a great addition to any family! Does he work
long hours, carefully weighing out precise one-ounce packets
of crank? Does he wait outside bars in his Mercedes SUV with
a baseball bat for his family's collection agency? Whatever
his characteristics, he's clearly fun. Enjoy! He's bringing a
long-overdue, dramatic, triangular element to you and your
sister's boring, resentful back-and-forth. Who cares whom

she "loves"? You do. Awesome. Go for it. Fight, manipulate, flirt with him and your sister! Let me know what happens!

Maria

...

Dear Maria:

I know that your age is just a number, but recently I feel like I'm becoming old. Not for the obvious reasons—going to sleep before 9:00 p.m., enjoying brunch specials, hating modern music—but because I'm pretty sure I'm shrinking. I saw it happen to my grandparents and parents, and now it's happening to me. Is there any way to reverse this process, or should I just check myself into a retirement community?

Jack P.
Brooklyn, NY

Dear Jack:

Get a wheelchair, a baked-potato-size dog, some sweatpants combos, and start really living! Gone are the isolation and self-consciousness of the middle ages. Fart, tell intimate stories to strangers, fly a Confederate flag on one side of your walker and a gay pride balloon on the other. Let go the constraints of youth. Embrace weakness, confusion, and simple woodworking projects. Our deepest fear is often our greatest wish. I congratulate you on your upcoming retirement.

Maria

...

Dear Maria:

At what point in a relationship is it appropriate to ask your spouse if he or she has a secret family in another state?

Worried in Denver, CO

Dear Worried:

I don't know how many times I need to say this. Enjoy! Your spouse and you share something very rare and special: a secret secret. Together you are building a legacy. That said, asking can be done at any time. And if it's done properly, it can even add to the fun! Here is a sample inquiry that you can use word for word or edit for your special case:

YOU: (*In a light, friendly tone, preferably at a relaxed time in the day, after dinner but not right before bed*) Cabbage Sweetie, I need to ask you something. And before I do, I just want you to know that I trust you implicitly and this is my "issue," not yours. I feel a little ashamed and silly for even asking, but here goes! (*Laugh.*) This is ridiculous. Okay, um, when you were in Las Vegas for the Best Practices conference at the Riviera? Right! And I was so glad that you called me and you told me about how that crazy rep from Chicago was getting on your nerves about how you need to change servers—that made me feel like you needed me and trusted my advice. Anyways, I was just looking at the Riviera's website (for fun) to see what the bad pool looked like that you described so hilariously, and by accident I saw that the Best Practices conference was in fact two weeks before, when you said your mom was sick and you had to drive up to Minneapolis. And here's the weird thing. I was taking out the trash—which I know you forgot to do and it's okay. No, it's fine! You've been busy!—and I find all these receipts and they're from the weekend you were supposed to be in Vegas, and they were from a few suburbs over from us, in Dearborn, and I thought, That's weird! One of them was for Applebee's with a pretty big total, like seven entrees with drinks. And another big tab was from Chuck E. Cheese and with your signature. So you know me; my mind is racing, putting all this stuff together like some crazy person, because my friend Judith said she saw this guy who looked just like you over in Dearborn that weekend but it was some guy who could've been your doppelgänger with four or maybe five or, well, let's just say a bunch of kids who looked just like our kids but different, I guess, and this woman, who looked a lot like me but she was Vietnamese, and Judith saw all of these people at this church where her sister goes. I don't know if you've met Judith. We met at Curves; she's so funny. So, this family, who of course had a different last name and all of that, but I guess this guy is pretty good at computer stuff and set up the church with a website and loves kids, is just like you. You're a great dad, by the way, if I haven't told you lately! So I just thought, What's going on here? Do you have a brother I've never met? And if so, I'd like to meet him. And if that's it, if you have a brother—and I'm not saying you do, but if you do—I want to meet him. Whenever you're ready, and of course, whenever he and his family are ready. I love you and, by association, I know I'll love your brother.

Maria

...

Dear Maria:

I'm thinking about having kids, but now I find out that by wearing "tightie-whities" rather than boxers for the past thirty years, I may have drastically reduced my sperm count. Is there a way of reversing the damage or am I doomed to a future of infertility?

Larry Jagodowski
Detroit, MI

Dear Larry:

First, get a lady friend or Fertile Myrtle. Then, have unprotected intercourse. Over and over again. Let me know what happens, but I think that should do the trick. Your future is bright.

Maria

Todd Barry

Dear Todd:
Is there anything—animal, vegetable, or mineral—that shouldn't
be used to make a bong?

Sincerely,
Fucked-up in the Northeast

Dear F.U.I.T.N.:
Rather than answer your question, I'd like to give a couple
of thank-yous. First, thank you for taking time away from
burning copies of the latest Moe album and writing me. Second, thank you for signing your letter "Fucked-up in the
Northeast." Most people who announce that they're "fucked-
up" aren't thoughtful enough to include the region of the
United States that they're "fucked-up" in. This is really handy
for travelers. Maybe some family is headed toward the Northeast. They don't want to expose their children to someone who

is "fucked-up"—even if that person is hilarious—so they now know that it is potentially safe to head northwest. (Although I've been there, and they have more than their share of people who are "fucked-up.") Anyway, to answer your question, I'm not a pothead but I'd probably make a bong out of any animal, any vegetable, but not the mineral wollastonite.

Todd

...

Dear Todd:
What's the difference between a transsexual and a transvestite? Which is the one where you tuck it instead of snip it? I just don't want to make a mistake that I'll regret for a long, long time.

Greg Sawyer
Macomb, MI

Dear Greg:
That's an easy one, Greg. A transvestite is someone you fuck. A transsexual is someone you marry.

Todd

...

Dear Todd:
I'm pretty sure that my girlfriend is cheating on me. I know this because I'm cheating on her and I've learned to recognize the signs. How can I expose her infidelity while protecting my own house of cards? (And please, no wise-ass "maybe you should stop cheating" advice. If I wanted a morality lecture, I would've asked my mom.)

Mr. Cake-and-Eat-It-Too
Savannah, GA

Dear Mr. Cake-and-Eat-It-Too:

It's really difficult to focus on your question with your girl-friend's lips around my cock. Not your mistress's lips. Your girlfriend's. I'm seriously involved in a torrid sexual relationship with your current girlfriend, and I'm actually having sex with her as I type this (selfish, I know). You want to expose her infidelity? Log on to my Flickr account and click the album titled *Mrs. Cake-and-Eat-It-Too.* Or, better yet, log on to her Photobucket account and click on the album titled *My Man-ah Who's Not from Savannah.* I could also e-mail you some evidence (unless you're one of those uptight assholes who "won't open anything with an attachment." Actually, scratch that. I'm one of those assholes). But to get back on track, your girlfriend is cheating on you. With me. Are we using protection? I don't know, are we? Let me check. Nope! No wonder it feels so extra good to have sex with your girlfriend.

Todd

...

Dear Todd:

When somebody tells me that I'm "balding gracefully," I can't help but think that they're secretly insulting me. For one thing, I'm confused by the word "balding." How can "bald" be a verb? I'm not actively doing anything. Balding is something that happens to you. I'm just standing there, watching my hair fall into the sink. And "gracefully" implies that it's some kind of physical performance. Somebody can do ballet gracefully, but balding—which, as I mentioned, isn't a real activity—doesn't possess any of the attributes that I usually qualify as grace. Maybe I'm just being overly sensitive, but I think my friends don't realize that using sloppy phrases like "balding gracefully" may not insult my vanity, but it does insult my intelligence.

Up My Own Ass?
Cleveland, OH

Dear Up My Own Ass?:
Yes.

Todd

...

Dear Todd:

I have a crush on Camille Paglia. At first it was just a silly fantasy, but now it's starting to affect my dating life. I broke up with my last girlfriend because she wouldn't deconstruct the cultural values placed on gender inherent in our lovemaking. I wish that were a joke, but it really isn't. Please help!

Bob
Santa Rosa, CA

Dear Bob:

I'll say to you what I say to all the young men who tell me they have a crush on Camille Paglia. Get in line. But seriously, Bob, I'm guessing that a guy who makes a Camille Paglia joke in 2009 should have his pick of women, perhaps even Ms. Paglia herself. Why don't you pursue her? I mean, she's alive and well and living in Philadelphia. Fly over there and hit her with that "deconstruct the cultural values" line. She'll melt like provolone on a cheesesteak. Make it happen, Bob.

Todd

...

Dear Todd:
I never thought I'd become that type of girl, but now it looks like I
might be. Does this happen to everybody or is it just me?
                                                    Lucy Franklin
                                                    St. Augustine, FL

Dear Lucy:
I wanted to give you an informed answer to your question, so
I decided to do a little fact-finding. I caught a red-eye to St.
Augustine, checked into a four-star hotel, and had the
concierge point me in the direction of the city's "hot spots."
The plan was to go to various bars and restaurants, meet
some locals, drop "Lucy Franklin" into the conversation,
then wait for a reaction. Based on your letter, I expected a
series of "Ooh, she's bad news" looks after uttering your
name. Instead, I got an onslaught of "You're barking up the
wrong tree if you think she's that type of girl" looks. I left
town before I was made to leave town. So that should make
you feel better. You are clearly not that type of girl.
    Hey, Lucy, I have a question for you: Why St. Augustine?
                                                    Todd

Samantha Bee

Dear Samantha:
I was wondering if you could give me some investment advice. I'm about to retire and I'm a little freaked.

Leah Dawson
Sarasota, FL

Dear Leah:
I'm freaked for you. I'm so freaked I don't even have any jokes. I was trying to think of a kind of jokey answer and then I just felt like a horrible person and I deleted it. I am really scared for you. Seriously scared. You are in serious trouble. I hope you've been hoarding conflict diamonds and Cipro, because you are about to enter the s-h-i-t, the Heart of Darkness. Take everything you ever thought you knew about investing and do the exact opposite. The currency of the future will be heirloom seeds, so good luck with that one. Panic. Learn how to field

dress a wild pig and distill your urine into potable water. Most important, if you take anything away from this response at all, just know that the best thing for you to do is to exercise a lot and stay really sinewy, so that when the cannibals come they will not want to eat you.

I should probably also mention that I just finished reading *The Road.* I don't know if that makes a difference at all.

Samantha

...

Dear Samantha:

I'm a youngish woman, neither gorgeous nor spectacularly ugly. If a dude shouts at me while I'm walking down the street, do I respond? I mean, it seems rude not to. When he just won't stop with the "Hey, babys," that must mean he really NEEDS me, right?

Good-looking Samaritan
New York, NY

Dear Good-looking:

I am appalled by your insensitivity. You mean you've been letting these poor dear gentlemen call after you in vain all this time? Maybe look down from your ivory tower once in a while and check out all the regular Joes on the ground floor. Guys who are married with kids but need nothing more than a quick hand release in a Port-O-Let from a woman who is neither gorgeous nor spectacularly ugly. Lonely fellows who could really use the soft touch of a youngish woman's hand as they crouch furtively behind the Dumpster at the 7-Eleven. Don't you understand how horny they are?!

Your Lady Flower is a gift to be shared with anyone who asks. Or shouts at you. Especially if they keep shouting at you. That's really macho.

Samantha

...

Dear Samantha:

I'm awesome. Sometimes I can't even deal with how awesome I am. The bigger problem is that I'm so awesome that other people don't want to be around me because they're jealous of my awesomeness. What's the most awesome way to approach my awesome problem?

Eileen Burke
Provo, UT

Dear Eileen:

Your name is very old lady–ish. There hasn't been a single Eileen born since 1935. In fact, the only Eileen I know is so old that her face is like a topographic map of the tribal regions of Pakistan. Also, as an old lady, maybe you can answer my question: Do old ladies really say "awesome"? Because there is nothing awesome about old age. Maybe nobody wants to be around you because all the other old ladies in your seniors' aqua-aerobics class don't understand your hip "lingo."

Thanks a lot. You just made me feel sad.

Samantha

...

Dear Samantha:

A few months ago I went into a store and found a cape for a baby with a lightning bolt on it. I thought it was funny and talked about it for a few days to various uninterested listeners. A few days later I found a passage about baby capes in the book I was reading. This is a lot of baby capes in my face all at once. Do you think God is trying to tell me to wear more baby capes?

Sandra
Miami, FL

Dear Sandra:

All those other listeners were right. This is uninteresting. When will you people ever learn that this is the kind of thing that can only be discussed on a blog, along with the content of your dreams, and other things that make you ROTFLMAO. The only thing God is trying to tell you is that you should start taking life seriously and stop dressing like Blossom.

Samantha

. . .

Dear Samantha:

Why, to put it delicately, does the carpet not always match the drapes?

Gavin Katz
Woodbury, MN

Dear Gavin:

Oh my god, did I just wake up in a 1970s porno? Nobody lays broadloom anymore; it's hardwood all the way. At the most you might put a runner down for a little traction, but that's it. Your question is irrelevant. You're like an adorable little anachronism. Did you type this question on your typewriter and send it in via pony?

Samantha

. . .

Dear Samantha:

I recently purchased some sea monkeys. On the booklet that accompanied the aquarium, it illustrates sea monkeys with the ability to dance, create government, and perform a plethora of other tasks. Unfortunately, my sea monkeys don't do anything but float in the aquarium. Is it outrageous to aspire for my pets to do things that other pet owners do with their pets?

                                 Christopher M. Lippa
                                 Brighton, MA

Dear Christopher:

You know what's so weird? I had the exact same problem when I recently purchased a cat! I was totally expecting her to create government and dance around, but all she did was float in the aquarium. Pets are useless. I think I might get a kid instead.

                                 Samantha

Michael Ian Black and Michael Showalter

Dear Michael and/or Michael:
My fiancée's father is pissed because I never asked him for permission to marry his daughter. But the last time I saw the guy, he took me aside and told me he was gonna slice my throat open the next time we were alone. Is there a polite way to make him feel involved in our wedding without giving him an opportunity to come after me with a hunting knife?

> *Scared Shitless Groom*
> *Evansville, IN*

Hi Shitless:
Sure, there are lots of ways to get on the old man's good side without worrying about being gutted like a fish. My suggestion: make him your DJ. You might be thinking he could still come after you with a record needle, but rest assured, modern DJs usually use either compact discs or MP3s.

There's very little danger involved, unless you dislike the singer Vic Damone, in which case the danger is very high.

Michael Ian Black

Dear Scared Shitless:

Michael Black really isn't the best authority on this sort of thing. His answer for everything is "Make him your DJ." What do I get my doorman for Christmas? Make him your DJ. How do I convince my boss to give me a raise? Make him your DJ. But DJs can't solve everything, Mike. Lucky for you, Shitless, I can relate to your specific situation. Funny story: when I proposed to my college girlfriend—well, before I proposed to my college girlfriend—I invited her father on an all-expenses-paid fishing tour of the Virgin Islands. Fantastic marlin out there. So, we're out in the middle of the big blue, slugging back Coronas on this yacht I rented with the last of my scholarship money, sun's setting, and I pull him aside and I say, "Dad," and then he says—this is the great part—"Dad?" Really high-pitched and adorable: "Dad?" And I say, "Yeah. I want you to be my dad. Dad." We've been best friends ever since. Girlfriend and I split that month, but Mr. Akers and I are as close as ever.

What was your question?

Michael Showalter

...

Dear Michael and/or Michael:

Who knew cashews were so high in carbohydrates? I mean, not like white-bread high but certainly higher than I thought. Are there any other foods deceptively high in carbs that might be sabotaging my diet?

Liz Fisher
Gaithersburg, MD

Dear Liz:

To answer this question fully and accurately, I'll need a photo of you. And another of you eating cashews.

Thanks!

Michael Showalter

Dear Liz:

Please disregard my friend Michael Showalter's coarse attempt at suavity. He cares little about the health ramifications of your cashew consumption. I, on the other hand, am concerned with your well-being. Now, I don't know what you're into, but jizz has a lot of carbs. People think sperm is just a great source of protein, and it is, but it's also loaded with carbs. The twist? They're the good kind of carbs. The baby-making kind.

Michael Ian Black

...

Dear Michael and/or Michael:

I went to dinner at my mom's place last weekend and she served something called "chicken à la king." I called her out on it. Isn't that like when fast-food restaurants call their ketchup "fancy"? So anyway, I said to my mom, "Chicken à la bullshit," and now she's not talking to me anymore. What should I do?

Sandra

Grand Rapids, MI

Dear Sandra:

Take a step back: What if people told you that what you liked to eat was "bullshit"? You'd probably feel pretty insulted, too. I guess my question to you is, why are you all up in your mother's shit? All she ever did was give birth to you and raise you the best she could. And then you turn around and throw it in her face. My advice: pick up the phone and apologize. You'll be glad you did.

Michael Ian Black

Dear Sandra:

Have you considered waterboarding? But seriously, have you? I think about it all the time.

Michael Showalter

...

Dear Michael and/or Michael:
As I've gotten older, my skin has become more sensitive and breaks out very easily. I've heard that a skin care regimen might help, but I don't have the attention span to slap on moisturizer every night. Is there an easier way to maintain youthful skin for us lazy girls?

Linda M.
Baltimore, MD

Hi Linda:

Absolutely. My once-a-month never-fails skin care regimen is sure to keep your skin as clear and supple as a new contact lens. On the first day of every month, dip six to eight aloe leaves in a mixture of one part lavender, one part red wine vinegar, and two parts maple syrup. Affix those leaves to your "problem areas" with surgical tape and voilà! You're done. Just keep those leaves where they are for the next four weeks until you're ready to do it all over again. Even if it doesn't clear up your skin, nobody will notice because you'll have aloe leaves all over your face.

Michael Ian Black

Dear Linda:

Black does have a knack for beauty chemistry, but I've taken our shared talent a step further and merchandised my personal at-home remedy. Go on, try Black's method—but what if you find your face still looks like a caprese salad? What then? You're in luck. My brand-new patent-pending formula is hitting your pharmacist's shelves as we speak: Michael Showalter's Baby Boot™. Made from the purest infant vomit, spit-up, and diarrhea, Michael Showalter's Baby Boot™ both smooths lined, wrinkly skin and soaks up excess bacteria and pus. Just dab a generous amount of this unique night cream onto problem areas and smack on that lipstick, girl! Your friends and/or sexual partners will be too distracted by the glistening slime and offensive odor to notice your repulsive acne sores.

   Good luck!

Michael Showalter

...

Dear Michael and/or Michael:
Can you substitute baking soda for baking powder?
Lauren M.
Manhattan, KS

Hi Lauren:
This sounds like the kind of question a terrorist would ask.
Michael Ian Black

Dear Lauren:
I revert to my standard motto: "No Substitutions—Genuine Class."

Michael Showalter

...

Dear Michael and/or Michael:
I'm almost seventy-four years old and my doctor just told me I have
genital warts. How the hell is that possible? I was in the military
and banged everything that moved, and I get my first STD when
I'm old as dirt? That can't be fair, can it?

The Colonel
West Palm Beach, FL

Dear Colonel:
You're right. It's not fair. And those who know Michael
Showalter know that I am a staunch advocate of our men in
uniform. That's why I'm sponsoring the Veterans of Foreign
Wars Gettin' Freaky Act. This bill will mandate that Uncle
Sam pay for that genital wart cream, the herpes antibiotics,
the sex-offender rehabilitation courses—whatever it is that
you need to keep on gettin' freaky. It's not a sexually transmitted disease—it's a sexually transmitted solution.

Patriotically yours,
Michael Showalter

Hi Colonel:
Michael Showalter may say he supports old people, but his
rhetoric ignores the cold hard facts: Michael Showalter just
doesn't like old people. I, however, *love* them, and I've
thought long and hard about your query, Colonel. Maybe
you sat on a very old toilet seat. That is the only possible
explanation. (Vote Michael Ian Black for mayor.)

Michael Ian Black

Andy Borowitz

Dear Andy:
I shave my head but I'm not bald. Nobody seems to believe me. When did a shaved head become the new comb-over?

Alex Sullivan
Cedar Rapids, IA

Dear Alex:
You raise an interesting historical question: When did a shaved head become the new comb-over? Certainly not in 1979, when Persis Khambatta played the shiny-pated Lieutenant Ilia in the first *Star Trek* movie and ignited no speculation about the plentitude of her follicles. Nor was it in the eighties and nineties, which spawned such high-profile cue balls as Sinéad O'Connor and Vin Diesel. I think you have to jump all the way to the early part of this century for your answer: the suspicious midlife

deforestation of Hollywood moguls Jeffrey Katzenberg and David Geffen.

Andy

...

Dear Andy:

I had an abortion last year and made the mistake of telling my mother. She told me that if Mary had an abortion, there never would've been a Jesus. I thought about it later and realized she's right. Long story short, my libido is gone. Any tips on how I can enjoy sex again?

Lindsay S.
Denver, CO

Dear Lindsay:

Generally speaking, it's hard to have an orgasm if you're thinking about Jesus, Mary, and your mother. I mean, I'm sure your mother is sexy in her own way, but you shouldn't be thinking about her if you're trying to come anytime soon. It sounds like you need a surefire turn-on to get back in the game. Have you ever done a guy with a shaved head? Let me know if you're interested and I'll hook you up.

Andy

...

Dear Andy:

I do all of my reading on the toilet, and because I prefer big, beefy novels, I guess I spend more time on the pot than some might consider healthy. As a result of my excessive bathroom visits, I've developed anal fissures. My wife thinks this is a bad thing, but as I've repeat-

edly reminded her, I'll gladly endure a little rectal burning if it means finally finishing Remembrance of Things Past. *What do you think?*

> *Brad Gregerson*
> *Greensboro, NC*

Dear Brad:
I sincerely hope that Lindsay S. of Denver, CO, did not read your letter. She's having enough trouble with her sex drive already without your planting these horrid images in her mind.

> Andy

. . .

Dear Andy:
My teacher says that the human body is 65 percent water. I don't think I believe him. If that's true, then why can't we breathe underwater? If we're half water, why does water kill us?

> *Scott, age 8*
> *San Antonio, TX*

Dear Scott:
You can't breathe underwater? Consult your physician immediately. You may be made of sand.

> Andy

. . .

Dear Andy:

My doctor says I have hippocampal sclerosis, but I don't know. It sounds like a fake disease. Is it for real?

> *Jennifer Bowden*
> *Jackson, MI*

Dear Jennifer:

According to Wikipedia, hippocampal sclerosis is a disease whose symptoms include "segmental loss of pyramidal neurons, granule cell dispersion and reactive gliosis." But I wouldn't be concerned if I were you—like most things on Wikipedia, it's probably all made up.

> Andy

...

Dear Andy:

Do you remember those comics, Classics Illustrated? Why did they stop making them? Because of CI, I can hold my head up high and say I've read The Iliad *and* Les Misérables. *But what about modern classics like . . . well, I don't know. Without comics, I'm lost.*

> *Eric Johnson*
> *Brooklyn, NY*

Dear Eric:

The demise of Classics Illustrated was indeed a negative development, and not just for posers like you. Since CI stopped publishing, the incidence of anal fissures in the United States has shot up 300 percent.

> Andy

...

Dear Andy:
What's another word for "gyneolatry"? I looked it up in the thesaurus
and couldn't find something that really captures the essence of it.

Tongue-tied in San Diego

Dear Tongue-tied:
"Insnatchuation."

Andy

Michael Cera

•

Dear Michael:
Do you think turtles tell jokes? It seems like they could be really funny.

> *Rilo*
> *Akron, OH*

Dear Rilo:
I think that turtles definitely do not tell jokes. They could still be funny, I think, but it would be purely based on their appearance and the way that they move really slowly. But if we scrutinize further, we find that the humor ends there, and the sadness of the turtle's existence washes away all the jokes, culminating as the ultimate truth of the animal.

> Michael

...

Dear Michael:
I am beginning to think the word "cobbler" can mean anything you
want it to. Person who mends shoes, deep-dish fruit dessert, rejected fab-
ric, or mummichog. Are we moving toward a new world where the only
word is "cobbler" and our only clues are inflection? How can I prepare?

Anonymous
Sedona, AR

Dear Anonymous:
It's an interesting point to bring up. Being a purist, I've
always referred to my mummichog as "mummichog," and
"mummichog" alone. I also tend to refer to people who
mend shoes as "feet-housers," and rejected fabric as "self." I
think we should be civilized and leave "cobbler" to the deep-
dish fruit dessert, as it's such a delicious, deep, fruity word to
say and hear and cobble.

Michael

. . .

Dear Michael:
In middle school my science teacher told me talking to plants helps
them grow. What do you think?

Sincerely,
I'd Rather Not Say

Dear I'd Rather Not Say:
I think there's a very good chance that your middle school
science teacher was a bonehead and was trying to impress
you by dangling a whole bunch of worthless knowledge in
your face.

Michael

. . .

Dear Michael:
Why is it that educated people are such assholes? I mean, they just looove to flaunt their trivial knowledge. It's like they want to impress everybody or something.

> Jason P.
> Warren, MI

Dear Jason:
Did you know talking to plants helps them grow?
> Michael

...

Dear Michael:
I think my landlady/downstairs neighbor may be selling crack out of her apartment. She also yells very loudly at her boyfriend around midnight every night, like clockwork, and makes the house shake with her incoherent, catlike rants. Also, her phone rings a lot. What do I do?

> J.J.
> Boulder, CO

Dear J.J.:
This one is simple. Befriend the boyfriend. B-friend the B-friend. Be a friend. Wait outside the place. When he leaves one day, be casually walking by. Say, "Hey, you live below me, right?" (He says yes) and you say, "Coffee?" (He says yes) and you go to a café and say, "What's your name anyhow?" (He tells you) and you say, "So, _____, how's life treating you?" (He says fine) and you say, "Fine is fine with me. Heck, fine is almost as good as good." (He laughs and smiles) and you say, "I really like making you laugh; we should hang out again soon." (He says for sure) and you say, "Can I come by and maybe borrow some crack, you think?" (He says sure,

you can take some, me and my girlfriend sell crack out of our apartment but we only have a little bit left but you can totally take it) and you say, "That'd be really great; I'd really appreciate that." (He says what's mine is yours) and now you have a new friend and an unbelievably convenient crack hookup, and next time you see him it wouldn't be weird or out of the blue for you to say, "Hey, I heard you guys arguing last night at midnight. Trouble in paradise?" and get the scoop on the yelling situation.

Michael

· · ·

Dear Michael:
I'm not sure what to do this weekend. Got any ideas?
Bored in San Antonio, TX

Dear Bored:
Here's what I think you should do: Go to the garden center and purchase some tree seeds (anything from an arroyo sweetwood to a western soapberry will do), and plant the seeds in your front yard. Wait patiently for the seeds to blossom into a beautiful baby tree (approximately two to three hours), and then talk to it. This will help the tree grow, as well as make it less lonely/bored.

Michael

· · ·

Dear Michael:
How is it that every time I go to the grocery store, I forget to get the milk?

Isadora
Modesto, CA

Dear Isadora:

You've just got way too much on your mind. You need to clear your head, girl. Spend a weekend in San Antonio; there's a ton of fun stuff to do there.

Michael

Vernon Chatman and John Lee

Dear Vernon and/or John:
Does electrolysis really work? I'm not so sure.

Angie Kritenbrink
Federal Way, WA

Dear Angie:
First off, what is Federal Way? That sounds like some sort of lie. There is no "way" for our federation. Like the Death Star or Rome, we are hurtling toward an abysmal destination that only the worthless history books and withered poets can encapsulate, word-wise. As for your question about electrolysis, try covering your hirsutitude with a hat, preferably worn faux-haphazardly askew, as is the style these days.

Vernon and John

...

Dear Vernon and/or John:
My nine-month-old pug named Fang has recently taken a liking to
eating his own poop. When I get the chance to actually spend an
entire day with him, I feel like he teaches me a thing or two. My
question is, should I try eating his poop?

Chris Funk
guitarist for the Decemberists
Portland, OR

Dear Chris:

Well, yours is an arrestingly unique conundrum, Mr. Funk. And, in fact, you very well may be joking, as is your human right. But we still intend to answer this question for the benefit of those for whom the nightmare of Spastic Fecal Ingestion is very real. SFI has only recently been acknowledged by the U.S. Medicalry Institute, an organization that itself has yet to be recognized by anyone anywhere. It just so happens that our great-aunt Lillia "suffered" your plight, but she was a fighter to the last who could beat anything, and she "passed" her homeliest of home remedies on to us. Use it wisely: take a quarter-pinch of raw talcum powder and hold it between your two ring toes; douse your back hair in a blend of rainwater, cran-apple cocktail, and Dramamine; pop the ticks on your left arm with a wooden matchstick, and, as they burst, kiss a jar of our grandmarm's famous hand-marmed marmalade between each of the crisp crackles, take a deep breath, hold it, and then immediately eat as much of the dog's rectal output as you can stomach. You should awake the next morning to find your hair has more bounce, more luster, and more sheen than you could have possibly foreseen!

Vernon and John

...

Dear Vernon and/or John:
Since arriving in New York about a year ago, I haven't been moti-
vated to cook. I haven't had sex, either, and I'm beginning to think
the two are somehow related. My friends have suggested the "pity
lay," but I feel that's cheating—sort of the equivalent of a
microwave dinner. Any suggestions for turning these two worrying
trends around?

> *Lauren Marks*
> *New York, NY*

Dear Lauren:
Manners! Never, ever, *ever* turn down a "pity lay." It is also
considered bad form to reject the offering of a courtesy cud-
dle, a grievance grope, sorrow sex, a hunger hump, a shame
shag, an ennui shower, a gloat scroting, a phantom-limb
handjob, an anosognosian booty call (with one's own booty,
no doubt), a gymnophobes dry hump, a rusty-trombone
marrow transplant, a free falafel (shoved up your ass), or a
sincere, sensual session of meaningful lovemaking.

As for your question, what you feel is natural. Food and
sex fit together like a penis made of olives fits into a snug
vagina knit from hen cutlets. Our advice is, be careful out
there. Don't want those olives to spoil. Always keep them in
chilled brine before serving (penetration).

> Vernon and John

...

Dear Vernon and/or John:
Why is it that every time my family sits down for a Sunday dinner
I simultaneously feel the urge to massacre each one of them with my
bare hands, ripping every fiber of their being into obliteration and
leaving no shred of evidence except for their as-yet-untouched plates
of barbecued chicken and mashed potatoes, which I will surely eat

*once I wash my hands of the evidence, and want to hug them until
they bleed?*

Ben Siegel
Williamsville, NY

Dear Ben:

You'll be happy to know that this is not your fault. The
only thing to blame here is that dastardly rascal known as
"your emotions." This horrible fiend has revealed the thin
double-edged sword between love and hate. Again, not your
fault. And fear not; we have a solution to your woes. But to
ensure that our advice isn't bogged down in crass feelings,
we have printed it in binary code: 101101001 10101
1010110110, 111 0010 101 0111. 1010 10101 10
01010101 1010 Coca-Cola 1010111 10101 1011 01
0101010 10101 . . . 0101 01.

Vernon and John

. . .

Dear Vernon and/or John:

*I am a forty-eight-year-old who has been enjoying the occasional use
of cannabis since puberty. Because this is an illegal substance con-
trolled by a mafia of seventeen-year-olds, I find that it has become
difficult (if not impossible) for a middle-aged suburbanite to hook
up with "the man." Should I just grow up and go cold turkey, or go
back to high school and hope to hang with a cool crowd? Please
advise.*

Theodore W. Oestendiek
A rural part of Arizona

Dear Theodore:
It is well-known that Rodney Dangerfield went back to
school for the same reasons you are thinking, and now he's

dead. Or, let's put it this way: It's like my beloved Aunt Clorvis always used to say. "Let me make this very clear. We are not related. Kindly remove your withered bodyclaw from my ladybags." In other words, follow your heart. But whatever you do, do it au gratin. And just in case you still missed it, let me dumb it down for you a notch: make like a fig and fuck off, stoner.

Vernon and John

Rob Corddry

Dear Rob:

I'm seriously considering buying a houseboat. I already know about all the bad reasons to do this—my friends and family have been very helpful in that department—but nobody has bothered to tell me why this would be insanely cool and bad-ass. What do you think?

Chad Lewis
Waukesha, WI

Dear Chad:

Just curious: What are the *bad* reasons to buy a houseboat? A deep, penetrating sleep cycle? Iconoclastic neighbors? Too much pussy? Unless you hate Halloween, I can't think of one single reason not to buy a sleek, modern houseboat. By the way, I'm cc'ing my houseboat salesman on this.

Rob

...

Dear Rob:
Will learning to juggle increase my chances with the ladies?
Ralph
Toledo, OH

Dear Ralph:
That you even have to ask is evidence that you are hopeless with "the ladies." I doubt it's your lack of carnival skills hurting you the most, my uncoordinated friend. Only we jugglers know the real secret to soaking a woman's panties: three balls and the truth.

Rob

...

Dear Rob:
The other day somebody asked me what my spirit animal is, and I honestly had no idea what to tell him. Where would I find this information? And do I get a say in the matter?
Brendan S. G.
Albuquerque, NM

Dear Brendan:
I will answer your question in the form of a story, not unlike the way Jesus would.

When I was a young man, I was an avid hiker. I would spend hours walking trails, communing with nature. It was there that I developed a profound communion with the residents of the forest. It was there that I felt I could communicate with them on some basic level. It was also there that I ate a poisonous mushroom and tripped my nuts off for days until the forest ranger found me living in a burned-out car surrounded by waterlogged *Playboy* magazines.

Long parable short, my spirit animal is Miss February 1986's vagina.

Rob

...

Dear Rob:

I am fairly reluctant to "dive in" when it comes to kitchen appliances, but maybe it's because nothing interesting enough has been produced yet. If you could crossbreed two kitchen appliances into one MEGA appliance, what would they be and what would you call it?

Just curious.

Mel in Chicago, IL

Dear Mel:

As a rich and famous person, all of my appliances are MEGA. It's a secret little perk, like being able to murder one person a year. My fridge doubles as an oven, so you can imagine the convenience there. My helper robot has most kitchen utensils readily available to me, and my coffeemaker doubles as a toilet. Oh, and I have slaves.

Rob

...

Dear Rob:

My roommate is a slob and he never pays his share of the rent or bills. But he's got an old record player and an amazing collection of vinyl, including a mint-condition copy of London Calling. *My question is, if I murder him will the records be taken away as evidence?*

Emma Lynsky
Fort Wayne, IN

Dear Emma:
I'm not sure I understand your logic. Do you usually make a habit of watching only half of *CSI*? I think the records would be admissible only if you killed him with them, which would be a fuller, warmer, crackly kind of murder. But also kind of elitist.

Rob

...

Dear Rob:
There's this shop around here that sells foofy stuff. Bells and whistles. Seashells, feathers, fancy cups. Absinthe. Gem-studded coasters. Dessert napkins. Lots of French imports. Should I feel guilty about buying things from there? Is it obvious that I only like this stuff because I'm being ironic? If not, how do I make my guests aware that I'm not the kind of guy who shops at foofy stores?

J. M. Barrie
San Francisco, CA

Dear J. M.:
The answer to your real question is yes, I do not like you.

Rob

...

Dear Rob:
They say bank heists are up this year. Do you recommend a life of crime or what?

> *My best,*
> *Parched in Houston*

Dear Parched:
Bank crimes are up this year, but the word "heist" is down. Keep beatin' your gums like a palooka and you'll be all fours and fives! Keep on the sinker and you'll be on the trolley like a hayburner!

I had to look all that stuff up but I got bored. "Sinker" means "doughnut." Yes, crime pays.

> Rob

...

Dear Rob:
What's the second-best way to ask your boss for a raise?

> *Lucy*
> *Tallahassee, FL*

Dear Lucy:
Assuming that the best way to ask your boss for a raise is to build a time machine, go back in time, fix all of your stupid mistakes, and start making good, responsible choices while being nice and respectful to your fellow workers? The second would be to just ask him.

> Rob

Larry Doyle

Dear Larry:

I have trouble making a good impression on new people. I cannot engage in an intelligent conversation for more than five minutes before I am suddenly, unnaturally aware that I am communicating and am doing it badly. How can I be more likable?

Sue
Stroudsburg, PA

Dear Sue:

Why do you want to be liked, Sue? You know who was liked? Adolf Hitler. One of Jessica Mitford's sisters even called him "sweet." And yet.

But if you still want to be liked, Sue, I would recommend that when meeting a new person, you try to maintain eye contact. And never, ever say anything stupid. Good luck!

Larry

...

Dear Larry:

This year I will be turning twenty-seven, which as we all know is the ripest age for suicide. Several of my friends have gone before me—to the age of twenty-seven, not suicide—and my time is fast approaching. I can't help but feel despair. Do you have any advice on how to cope with the post-twenty-seven, suicide-free, life-after-death lifestyle?

Wendi
Cleveland, OH

Dear Wendi,

There's no way to make it past twenty-seven without committing suicide and not feel somewhat a failure. After that magical age, one risks ending a life no longer worth living, undermining the romance of it all. Hemingway blew his brains out at sixty-one, depriving the world of what? A thousand-page, slightly more pornographic *Garden of Eden?*

Wendi, you are right to stick with your plan. Your post-suicidal friends will try to talk you out of it, but in the end they will admire your gumption, so tragically self-snuffed.

Larry

...

Dear Larry:

My white-ass friend and my own white ass were walking by the lake the other day, and after I told her a joke she screamed, "You a jive-ass turkey!" Loudly. A black guy whom I hadn't noticed jogging in front of us turned around abruptly with a really weird look on his face. Should I try to make my friend feel bad about that or was this man just being oversensitive?

White and Uptight
Minneapolis, MN

Dear White and Uptight:
I'm afraid you lost me at "my white-ass friend." This kind of indecorous anatomical reference I would expect from an Urban Person, not a Minnesotan.

Larry

...

Dear Larry:
I'm one of those naïve young people who still dream of writing the Great American Novel. Am I wasting my time? Is the novel dead, as so many of my peers have told me, or is there still hope that I might become an acclaimed and award-winning author?

D. R. Sullivan
Cambridge, MA

Dear D. R.:
Your little friends are wrong. They have been affected by the skepticism of a skeptical age. They think that nothing can be which is not comprehensible by their little minds.

Yes, D. R., the Great American Novel lives. It exists as certainly as love and generosity and devotion exist, and you know that they abound and give to your life its highest beauty and joy. Not believe in the Great American Novel! You might as well not believe in short stories or writers' retreats!

Larry

...

Dear Larry:

I had insomnia a few nights ago and I ended up watching the "Sixth Finger" episode of The Outer Limits. *It occurred to me that this episode is a perfect metaphor for anti-intellectualism. Is this how people in the red states look at the rest of us, as translucent aliens with huge brains?*

> *Bryan H.*
> *Scottsdale, AZ*

Dear Bryan:

I am not allowed in red states, so I cannot answer your question knowledgeably, but I'm happy to speculate on what other people think. I doubt that they view you as a more highly "evolved" species, though I'm sure that watching something in black-and-white, even on TV, makes you suspect. Meanwhile, watching television, even ironically, makes you unfit to walk among your own. You are a man without a half-a-country.

> Larry

...

Dear Larry:

I have a mole on my cheek with irregular edges that my husband thinks might be melanoma. But I'm afraid of going to a dermatologist and letting him hack it off, because my mole is one of the most interesting things about my face. Isn't being unique worth a little skin cancer?

> *Cheri Colvin*
> *Rochester, NY*

Dear Cheri:

Of course. However, you may want to consider how interesting your face will look with a big hole in it.

> Larry

...

Dear Larry:
All of us up here in Canada are a little nervous about what you guys in the United States are up to. You're not planning to invade us anytime soon, are you? Just give us a heads-up; that's all we're asking.

> *Cheers,*
> *Brigette K.*
> *Winnipeg, MB, Canada*

Dear Brigette:
No, not at all. Please continue disarming your populace and emasculating your men with draconian pornography laws.

> Larry

Paul Feig

Dear Paul:
I just had a dream where a large bear started attacking me because
I was in a prison tower and it was angry. I am concerned because in
the dream, someone I don't know brought the bear to my house in a
plastic igloo and said, "Look, it's my pet!" Is this an omen?
                                              Liz, age 18

Dear Liz:
What kind of a bear was it? Grizzly? Polar? Teddy? Chicago?
What kind of prison tower? An old one, like the Tower of London? Older, like the one Rapunzel tossed her hair out of? Or
modern, like the kind the guards stand on at San Quentin?
And what kind of igloo was it? One of those doghouse igloos?
If so, the bear couldn't have been that big. It wasn't an Igloo-
brand cooler, was it? The bear would be even smaller if that
was the case. If you want my help, I need details, girl. Maybe

you eighteen-year-olds think this whole vague-description thing is the bomb, but for us guys in our forties, we need specifics. You wouldn't be this ambiguous if I were Dr. Phil, now would you? Write me back and get that thesaurus out.

Paul

. . .

Dear Paul:

For years I have tried to make my Hungarian grandmother's cucumber salad. She improvises her recipe, so she wrote down the steps for me to follow. But try as I might, mine never tastes as good as hers. What am I doing wrong?

Linda Nagy
Fort Wayne, IN

Dear Lisa:

You're trying to crash your grandmother's party, that's what you're doing. Did you ever stop and think that maybe your grandmother isn't giving you the exact recipe because she wants your salad to be worse than hers? What's next? You going to try on her clothes? Steal her boyfriend? Pretend that you're from Hungary, too? My advice is to let your grandmother be the master of her cucumber recipe. Tell her she's the only one who can make it, then take a bowl of it to a lab and have it analyzed. Then you can make the exact recipe in the privacy of your home and she'll still believe she's the queen of the cucumbers.

Paul

. . .

Dear Paul:

I am twenty-five years old, but people often mistake me for a seventeen-year-old. I wouldn't mind so much if it meant I was getting discount bus fare, but it's all the wrong people who think I'm a minor. Do I have to wear makeup and shave my legs to be taken seriously?

> *Lisa*
> *St. Louis, MO*

Dear Lori:

Get out a piece of paper and write down the pros and cons of being mistaken for a seventeen-year-old. Cons: you get carded at bars and 7-Elevens, your parents still feel like they can treat you like a child, and high school guys hit on you. Pros: you're always going to look younger than you are, you can act like a teenager and no one will tell you to "grow up," and you can help out in that *To Catch a Predator* program by luring creepy Internet stalkers into the house so Chris Hansen can come out with his cameramen and humiliate the pervy perpetrators.

I'd say the pros list wins. Relax and enjoy your perpetual youth.

> Paul

...

Dear Paul:

Please provide your insight to the following two topics:

The bikini line (bacon strip)—shave or wax?

Lathering up in the shower—washcloth, loofah, or direct application of soap?

> *Annette Fletcher*

Dear Annette,

First of all, let me say what a pleasure it is to answer a question from someone whose name does not begin with an L. Second, do you really think I'm gonna tell you how to run your genital life? How can I possibly win at that game? I say, "Sure, shave away!" You get out the old Lady Schick and sneeze at an inopportune moment, and the next thing I know I'm sitting in court being sued for destruction of property. I say, "Hey, wax that thing!" You head to the salon, the beautician had greasy French fries at lunch, the hot wax container slips out of her slippery fingers just as she's attending to your lady parts, and the next thing I know I'm back in court getting sued like McDonald's did when that old lady dropped a cup of hot coffee on her hoo-ha. No way, Annette. I ain't playin' that game.

As for your lather question, I say cut out the middleman. You've got a bar of soap, you've got your body. The loofah will eventually get moldy and disgusting, and you'll have to wash the washcloth after you wash yourself with it, which is just so inherently redundant that it makes the very concept of the washcloth as sensical as a bathing suit that's "dry clean only." Use your hands the way our ancestors did.

Oh, one more thing—"bacon strip"?

Paul

...

Dear Paul:
My girlfriend's birthday is coming up in two weeks, and I only have five bucks to my name until I get paid next month. Any ideas?

Jay
Oakland, CA

Dear Jay:

You poor bastard. Literally. Five bucks until next month's paycheck? I know the economy is bad but yikes. What your girlfriend needs for her birthday is a new boyfriend with a better-paying job. I'm just kidding. Hittin' you with a little tough love because even though I've only known you for five seconds, you're like a son to me. You sound like a good, earnest guy and the fact that you would spend your last five dollars on a present for your girlfriend and not something crazy like food or paying your electric bill makes me want to help you out. I'd say take that five bucks to an office supply store, buy a hundred sheets of paper; a roll of tape, and a Magic Marker, write "Happy Birthday (your girlfriend's name)!" on each of the hundred pieces of paper, and then tape the papers all along the route your girlfriend takes to work in the morning. She'll love the gesture and if she doesn't, well, then break up with her. She's not worth spending your hard-earned cash on.

Feig out!

Jim Gaffigan

Dear Jim:
I once had a guy tell me that I looked like a beautiful picnic table.
What do you think this means? And should I be okay with it?
                                        Sally Teiman
                                        Chicago, IL

Dear Sally:
I don't know if I would ever characterize a picnic table as
beautiful really. Functional? Yes. Large? Yes. Hard to move?
Definitely. Beautiful? Not really. I don't know if this is a
compliment unless your legs are large wooden planks or
the guy who gave the compliment has a history of killing
women and turning them into lawn furniture.

   I'm curious. When you got this compliment were you by
chance standing in a park near, say, a picnic table? Sally,
sometimes things are not just about you. I know it sounds

crazy. Sometimes people can have strong feelings for things, not "Sally."

Jim

...

Dear Jim:
I was in Oklahoma a few months ago and I ordered the "vegetable of the day" for lunch. They brought me a dumpling with a side of macaroni and cheese. I was previously unaware that either of these items was in the vegetable family. What else classifies as a vegetable in Oklahoma?

Ashley
Eugene, OR

Dear Ashley:
How is the weather up there on your high horse? As far as I know restaurant menus in Oklahoma are not determined by the state government. I'm pretty sure they never were. I suppose the notion of the "vegetable of the day" in Oklahoma is pretty funny. Ha, ha, ha. Kind of like a good hamburger in India or a non-snobby Ashley in Oregon.

Jim

...

Dear Jim:
I have a tiny, almost unnoticeable Armani symbol on the side of my glasses. Does that make me a tool? I mean, my thick-rimmed glasses are really sweet.

Chad
San Francisco, CA

Dear Chad:

Unfortunately your glasses have nothing to do with making you a tool. If it were only the glasses then I suppose this could be solved. Sadly, I think it might have something to do with your first name, Chad. Unless your parents emigrated from Chad and named you in honor of their homeland, I can see no reason to name a child Chad.

I guess if your last name were Armani, you could say, "Hey, it's my last name. I'm Chad Armani." Admit it. Seeing "Chad" next to "Armani" really makes you realize how bad your first name is.

Jim

...

Dear Jim:

I had a weird dream last night where I went on a killing spree, murdering all of my ex–college roommates (I had a lot of them apparently), and for some reason Elvis Costello was fingered for the crime. I sat in the courtroom and watched him get a life sentence, and then he turned to me and smiled and started singing, "Alison, I know this world is killing you." And the really bizarre part is, my name isn't Alison. What could this dream mean?

Norah
Lancaster, PA

Dear Norah:

Wait—the "bizarre part" was that your name isn't Alison? Really, THAT was the bizarre part? Not the murder spree or your letting a great musician take the heat? Just your name? Lady, you are a nut bag. Stop watching *Law & Order* before bed.

Jim

...

Dear Jim:
What's the difference between extra-virgin olive oil and the regular kind?

> *Cindy, rocking it in Reno*

Dear Cindy:
I don't have time to do research, but I think the biggest difference between extra-virgin olive oil and virgin olive oil is that extra-virgin olive oil has an extra word. The word is "extra." That's probably it. Well, maybe when they create or make virgin olive oil there is leftover or extra-virgin olive oil? That could be. Why are you asking me? Just 'cause I own a dozen olive farms and I'm a virgin?

> Jim

...

Dear Jim:
I saw a sticker on a street pole the other day that read, CRAP!
OBAMA IS A MARXIST! *Should I be alarmed?*

> *Bryan Geoff Schuler*
> *Dallas, TX*

Dear Bryan:
Uh, yeah! They did use the word "crap." For someone to use such a crass word as "crap," I think it's pretty serious. I hope you crossed out "crap" and wrote "darn" or "by golly." Thank god kids can't read today or they would be totally corrupted by such language.

   By the way, who is Obama? I hope he's not black.

> Jim

...

Dear Jim:
Am I the only one in the world whose eyes are being fried by staring
at the computer so much? I hate to complain, but, yeah. I'm gonna.
Can I get goggles for this shit somewhere?

Max in Montana

Dear Max:
Sorry, we are all out of goggles here, but I'll see if I can send
over a really big crib so you can take a nap. I guess I should
just talk to your dad about paying for it. Enjoy your Winnie
the Pooh blanket.

Jim

...

Dear Jim:
My best friend's been turning into a real ass lately. Says he's been
getting migraines. I think it's the recession. We need marriage coun-
seling, except not for married people. Where do friends go for that
sort of thing? Or better yet, what's your ten-step recovery program for
friends on the rocks?

David V.
Pasadena, TX

Dear David:
Let me be clear up front. Your letter reminded me why I hate
all sitcoms about groups of friends. Now back to you. I must
admit you sound like a really great friend.

DAVID: How's it going?

FRIEND: Unfortunately, I have another really bad migraine.

DAVID: You're turning into an ass.

I suppose if your friend got a terminal disease you might want to sue him. Heck, you should be counseling people on sensitivity. Please accept my friend request.

Jim

Zach Galifianakis

Dear Zach:

Two years ago, I was married impetuously, against the wishes of my parents. Now everyone's content; that is, everyone but me. Lately I've noticed that my life is extremely dull. My friends no longer want to hang out since I've stopped drinking all the time. I'm boring! What can I do to quash this, and is this a normal rite of passage?

Jenny Skytta
Seattle, WA

Dear Jenny:
After long thought and looking up the word "impetuously," I have come to my answer. Dorothy Parker once said, "The cure for boredom is curiosity. There is no cure for curiosity." I think it is time to be curious about drinking again.

Zach

...

Dear Zach:
A friend recently gave me a twice-used Weber grill for my birthday.
The instructions are fairly clear that it is only to be used outdoors.
I never leave the house, however, because my neighbors are all govern-
ment spies. Is there a way that I can enjoy the delicious taste of
charcoal-grilled meat within the confines of my sanctum?

Brooke James Saucier
Evanston, IL

Dear Brooke:
So the government is hassling you, huh? Not surprising. I
get followed all the time because I wrote a memo to my
assistant saying that I used to date Dakota Fanning, and the
Bureau of Alcohol, Tobacco, Firearms and Explosives thinks
it's their business. Anyway, as for your question, grilling
inside is dangerous but rewarding. I usually grill in the
bathroom, since it's the only room with a built-in fan. Sitting on the toilet while checking the progress of your wiener
is a Fourth of July tradition in the Galifianakis home.

Zach

...

Dear Zach:
Why do stalkers usually chase people into abandoned amusement
parks?

Craig Baird
Memphis, TN

Dear Craig:
I think they're just following federal law. "Those wishing to
stalk or harass a fellow citizen by trailing them must eventu-

ally end up in an abandoned amusement park, a burned-out Taco Bell, or a docked retired naval battleship" (Sec. 18 U.S.C. 875c). Some states require stalkers to have a limp. In New Hampshire, you can't stalk anyone unless your name is Marcus.

Good luck.

Zach

...

Dear Zach:
I've been out of rehab for a while, and I've successfully replaced my drug addiction with a gambling addiction, but I'm still having trouble feeling at ease in society without the use of narcotics. Any suggestions?
Lorelei Leslie
Santa Monica, CA

Dear Lorelei:
The transition from rehab to the normal world is a tough one. I spent some time in rehab for my addiction to homemade Ecstasy—made from Tide with Bleach and some old Altoids. Somersaults in the park while singing any Spin Doctors song are also useful.

Zach

...

Dear Zach:
I am in the unfortunate position of having a receding hairline, but only on the right side of my head, giving me a half widow's peak. My wife says it makes me look unique, but I have become quite anxious about it. Should I shave the other side to match? Shave it all off? Wear a selection of hats?
Tim Matthews
London, England

Dear Tim:

I would definitely go with the hat. May I suggest a ski mask? Or a fez? Or both.

Zach

...

Dear Zach:

I have a job that leaves me passionless and empty. It stimulates neither mind nor soul. How can I successfully draw on my creative juices to do something meaningful?

Best,
Charles
Address withheld

Dear Charles:

Are you an accountant at a cardboard box factory? Boredom is a killer. There are so many things you can do to kick-start a satisfying life. I will give you a few suggestions to get the juices flowing:

1) Start reading *Teen People.*

2) Rent a stretch Hummer to go see Noam Chomsky speak.

3) Model your life after the movie *Sideways,* but instead of wine make your passion Mountain Dew.

4) Ask a state trooper where the closest gay bar is.

5) Have a Super Bowl party with no television.

Zach

...

Dear Zach:

My girlfriend and I have been together for about two months. The relationship is still new, but I think we're going to be together for a

*while. Some days she has a mustache, though. It's light and wispy
and makes me want to die. Is there any subtle, safe way to alert her
to her own facial hair and make her get rid of the mustache?*
                                               Eddie Turner
                                               Atlanta, GA

Dear Eddie:

I know what you're feeling. I date a Jewish girl with a Hitler
mustache and I've never said anything to her. I even bought
a biography of Frida Kahlo and pretended to read it while
my girlfriend looked on. I just shook my head and muttered,
"Can you believe this woman?" It went right over my girlfriend's mustached head. Now, I'm not normally one to recommend roofies, but sometimes they can help. Do I need to
say anything else?

                                               Zach

                          . . .

Dear Zach:

*I live in a medium-to-small one-and-a-half-bedroom apartment and
have the unfortunate habit of flea-market-find collecting. I am especially drawn to vintage celebrity dolls and action figures as well as
'60s barware. While my apartment is not yet to the point of being
overstuffed, it is threatening to happen any minute. Do you have any
suggestions for displaying my finds comfortably in my limited space?*
                                               Darwin Bell
                                               San Francisco, CA

Dear Darwin:

I, too, live in a small place that at least has high ceilings—or
they may be low floors; it's hard to say. My place is overflowing with Malcolm-Jamal Warner memorabilia, so I know
what you're going through. If you're living with someone,
maybe you could kick them out to make room for your stuff.

After I moved my grandparents into mini-storage, I was able to move around more freely.

Zach

...

Dear Zach:

My high school French teacher once told our class that French people hate root beer because "it tastes of medicine." Additionally, an Indian friend of mine claims that Indians despise most cheeses, especially ricotta cheese, "because of the texture." I enjoy cooking international dishes for my international friends, but now I'm worried I might inadvertently make someone gag. Are there other "Food Prejudices from Around the World" I should know about?

Tiffany Lee-Youngren
San Diego, CA

Dear Tiffany:

During my worldly travels, I have experienced a couple of cultures with mysterious food turnoffs. For one, I know that many Hindus will not eat pizza with buffalo wings as a topping. I also know of a town in Wales where it's illegal to eat a foot-long hot dog because of the fear that someone might say, "I would like to have a foot-long inside me right now."

Zach

Janeane Garofalo

Dear Janeane:
My boyfriend hasn't had a job in three years. But he's a pretty boy,
very easy on the eyes. Is it worth keeping him around anyway, like
a lamp that's long since stopped working but you don't throw away
because it goes with the furniture?

Susan M.
Richmond, VA

Dear Susan:
The lamp provides you with a convenient place to hang
damp laundry. The boy without a job does not. The lamp
complements your home's decor. The lad on the dole does
not. If you are able to fuck the lamp, then you must donate
the boy to the Salvation Army. Get a receipt for tax purposes.

Janeane

...

Dear Janeane:
I'm thinking about getting a tattoo, but I want something that isn't
quite such an urban hipster cliché. Maybe something literary? Is
having a paragraph from Atlas Shrugged *tattooed on my back cool*
and unique, or just pretentious? I'm not sure.

> Julia Rockson
> Atlanta, GA

Dear Julia:
It is only "cool" if you allow room for an additional tattoo
that decries the cynical bastardization of Ayn Rand's philos-
ophy of rational self-interest by the conservative think-tank
movement.

> Janeane

...

Dear Janeane:
I know there's a difference between stalking and being romantically
attentive, but I can't figure out what it is. Please advise.

> Regards,
> Paul
> St. Louis, MO

Dear Paul:
It all depends on how good-looking you are. "Stalkers" tend
to be similar in appearance to people who saw *Cats* on Broadway more than forty-seven times. "Romantically attentive"
describes people who don't look like they've seen *Cats* on
Broadway more than forty-seven times.

> Janeane

...

Dear Janeane:
My hair is starting to go gray, but I can't tell if it makes me look
distinguished or like one of those hippie ladies who wear sandals
and teach pottery classes. What should I do?

Mrs. Larkin
Melbourne, FL

Dear Mrs. Larkin:
If you don't have the silver fox appeal of a James Brolin or a
Fionnula Flanagan, then you must work in concert with des-
tiny. Straddle that pottery wheel like you mean it!

Janeane

...

Dear Janeane:
I've been a smoker for thirty years, and I know I should probably
quit. But I don't want to satisfy those pricks who are always obnox-
iously preaching to me about cancer and coughing every time I light
up. Is there a not-so-unhealthy-but-equally-annoying habit I could
pick up that'd allow me to live longer while continuing to piss off the
right people?
    Thanks for your help.

Jason S.
Owensboro, KY

Dear Jason:
Join the Republican party. Do what they tell you.

Janeane

...

Dear Janeane:
I went to a swap meet where I cut my leg on some rusty scrap metal.
I don't remember the last time I had a tetanus shot. It hurts and
there is blood. Should I buy the mannequin arm or the Marky Mark
coffee mug?

Maggie Faris
St. Paul, MN

Dear Maggie:
The three-foot Mr. Peanut icon is a better buy. After you
leave the swap meet, put the oversize peanut in the car.
Drive to the nearest apothecary. Squeeze a dollop of
Neosporin from the tube onto your leg. (You don't need to
buy the salve.) Exit the pharmacy. Drive home. Install the
large peanut in your bedroom. Throw damp laundry over it.

Janeane

. . .

Dear Janeane:
My dad, whom I haven't seen in almost two decades, suddenly
turned up on my doorstep the other day. He wants to make up for lost
time and have the father-daughter relationship he denied me as a
girl. Is there a nice way to tell him, "You're my dad, I love you, but
buying a My Pretty Pony for a twenty-eight-year-old woman isn't
sweet, it's just kinda creepy and sad"?

Regards,
Anonymous

Dear Anonymous:
You now have the perfect opportunity to utter, "Father, don't
darken my doorstep again!" I envy you. Most people don't
even have a doorstep.

Janeane

Daniel Handler

Dear Daniel:
Now that we have a black president, is it okay to be a racist
again?

> Terry R.
> Eureka, CA

Dear Terry:
No.

> Love,
> Daniel Handler

...

Dear Daniel:
My grandpa was just laid off from a major car manufacturer. Do
you have any suggestions for work for the elderly? I don't want him

lazing around the house, driving my grandma crazy. He is a grouch.

> *Peter*
> *Austin, TX*

Dear Peter:
Dog walker.

> Love,
> Daniel Handler

...

Dear Daniel:
Do you have any tips on getting rid of a gopher infestation?
> *A.C.*
> *A part of Indiana you wouldn't know*

Dear A.C.:
Move.

> Love,
> Daniel Handler

...

Dear Daniel:
I can't enjoy cream soups anymore without thinking of that nasty Asian fetish. You know. Rhymes with "your latke" or "Milwaukee." Are there any tricks to eating a delicious cream of broccoli soup without being totally grossed out?
> *Rocky*
> *Gaithersburg, MD*

Dear "Rocky":
Tabasco.

>Love,
>Daniel Handler

...

Dear Daniel:
Are there any good reasons to be proud of my Norwegian heritage,
besides that John Lennon song?

>*A Man Without a Country*

Dear Man Without a Country,
Kristin Lavransdatter.

>Love,
>Daniel Handler

...

Dear Daniel:
My boyfriend wants us to move into a geodesic dome. I understand
that the real estate market is unpredictable and scary these days, but
I still don't think that justifies living in a huge soccer ball. What
do you think?

>*Call me "Nancy"*
>*Winnipeg, MB, Canada*

Dear "Nancy":
"Cool."

>Love,
>Daniel Handler

...

Dear Daniel:
I've been walking around in hundred-degree-plus heat and I can't find my car. It's a dark green '97 Camry, and the parking lot outside Ross is frickin' huge. Plus there's strawberry ice cream in the trunk.

Mario M.
Gillette, WY

Dear Mario:
Huh.

Love,
Daniel Handler

...

Dear Daniel:
How can you break up with your boyfriend in a way that tells him, "I don't want to sleep with you on a regular basis anymore, but please be available for late-night booty calls if I run out of options"?
Lily
Charlotte, NC

Dear Lily:
The story's so old you can't tell it anymore without everyone groaning, even your oldest friends with the last of their drinks shivering around the ice in their dirty glasses. The music playing is the album everyone has. Those shoes, everybody has those same shoes on. It looked a little like rain so one person brought an umbrella, useless now in the starstruck cloudless sky, forgotten on the way home, which is how the umbrella ended up in her place anyway. Everyone gets older on nights like this.

And still it's a fresh slap in the face of everything you had going, that precarious shelf in the shallow closet that will certainly, certainly fall someday. Photographs slipping into a crack to be found by the next tenant, that one squinter third from the left laughing at something your roommate said, the coaster from that place in the city you used to live in, gone now. A letter that seemed important for reasons you can't remember, throw it out, the entry in the address book you won't erase but won't keep when you get a new phone, let it pass and don't worry about it. You don't think about them; "I haven't thought about them in forever," you would say if anybody brought it up, and nobody does.

You think about them all the time.

Close the book but forget to turn off the light, just sit staring in bed until you blink and you're out of it, some noise on the other side of the wall reminding you you're still here. That's it, that's everything. There's no statue in the town square with an inscription with words to live by. The actor got slapped this morning by someone she loved, slapped right across the face, but there's no trace of it on any channel no matter how late you watch. How many people— really, count them up—know where you are? How many will look after you when you don't show up? The churches and train stations are creaky and the street signs, the menus, the writing on the wall, it all feels like the wrong language. Nobody, nobody knows what you're thinking of when you lean your head against the wall.

Put a sweater on when you get cold. Remind yourself, this is the night, because it is. You're free to sing what you want as you walk there, the trees rustling spookily and certainly and quietly and inimitably. Whatever shoes you want, fuck it, you're comfortable. Don't trust anyone's directions. Write what you might forget on the back of your hand, and slam down the cheap stuff and never mind the bad music from the window three floors up or what the boys shouted from the car nine years ago that keeps rattling in your head, because you're here, you are, for the warmth of someone's wrists where the sleeve stops and the glove doesn't quite begin, and the slant of the voice on the punch line of the joke and the reflection of the moon in the water on the street as you stand still for a moment and gather your courage and take a breath before stealing away through the door. Look at it there. Take a good look. It looks like rain.

Love,
Daniel Handler

Todd Hanson

Dear Todd:
We generally refer to tissues as Kleenex and gelatin as Jell-O.
I know there's a name for this. Is it synecdoche?
> *An English professor with too much time on his hands*
> *New Haven, CT*

Dear English professor with too much time on his hands:
What a fascinating question! As a matter of fact, the—hey, wait a minute . . . I just put two and two together here and am beginning to smell a great big rat! If you are (as you claim) an English professor, that means you are one of that rarefied strata of the intelligentsia who have access to buildings called "libraries," containing books known as "dictionaries." If so, you would have easily been able to sneak in and look up the definition of "synecdoche" yourself during the ample free time you claim to have on your hands.

If not, however, then you obviously don't (as, again, you claim) actually have too much time on your hands after all! Either way, you are revealed as a liar, right here in front of the entire readership of *The Believer*, all of whom, ironically, are now filled with *disbelief*.

By the way, that part of the second sentence? Where I likened the solution of a math problem to the detection of an odor? That's called a mixed metaphor. Look it up, Socrates!

Todd

. . .

Dear Todd:
I don't care about politics. I really just care about everyone shutting the hell up. Does that make me a douche?

Hallie
San Francisco, CA

Dear Hallie:
Considering that a healthy democracy depends on an informed and involved populace, yes, technically, that does make you a douche. But god bless you for being an honest douche!

Considering all the not-shutting-the-hell-up involved in the last presidential election—which began more than two and a half years before the election itself, and of which only approximately 2 percent was remotely relevant to said election (the parts that happened in the last two weeks or so before November 4)—I think the sentiment of wanting everybody to shut the hell up is something anybody, including me, can relate to in a big way.

So let me doff my hat to you, Hallie! You are the only one with the courage to say what we all are feeling!

But again, yes, technically you're a douche.

Todd

...

Dear Todd:

I've been thinking it over a lot. Astronauts have become much less popular in recent years, and I'm guessing they figured this would happen from the get-go, because, in hindsight, how could you not? Anyways, assuming they've probably pulled the wool over our eyes out of spite, what should we believe about the moon and outer space?

> *Graciously,*
> *Simon Koppler*
> *Lexington-Fayette, KY*

Dear Simon:

You are needlessly overcomplicating things. Ask yourself this one simple question: Does the Bible say anything about the moon and outer space? The answer is yes—about three sentences' worth. It mentions something vague about a firmament and then something about a light in said firmament to shine during the night. And that's all it says. And therefore, that's all we need to know about it. As the Upright Citizens Brigade has been saying for more than ten years now, astronauts can go fuck themselves. Take that, science!

> Todd

...

Dear Todd:

I always thought I was emo, but according to my friends, I'm more goth. Why could this be? Is it the mascara? Aren't emo kids allowed to wear makeup occasionally?

> *Brad*
> *Evanston, IL*

Dear Brad:

I'm really glad you asked that question, because I myself have been struggling with the distinction between emo and goth for years now. From what I can tell in my old age, the emotions expressed are essentially the same, except goth sounds delicate and fey, like the farts of winged fairies, and emo is raw and loud, like two trucks fucking. Both seem to involve a mascara option, so I can't help you there. But let me ask you this: Do you have forearm tattoos? That could put you over the fence to emo right there. And if, conversely, you have a parasol made of black lace that you carry on sunny days, you're probably goth. Sorry I couldn't be of more help there, Brad. In either case, you should seriously consider dropping the name "Brad."

                                                    Todd

                                    ...

Dear Todd:

Obviously, hooking up with your cousin is a bad idea, as in your first cousin. But what about your second cousin? That's allowed, right?

                                    J.J. in Carson City, NV

Dear J.J.:

Again we're gonna have to go with the Bible on this one. Considering that all humans descended from one original Adam and Eve pairing, it would appear that all forms of incest are perfectly acceptable. Hook up with your cousins all you want!

                                                    Todd

Tim Heidecker and
Eric Wareheim

Dear Tim and/or Eric:
I really want to fight a bear. How can I make this happen?
                                      Thomas
                                      Saginaw, MI

Dear Thomas:
Is you what? This has to be a joke question. Why would you want to fight a bear? You could get hurt! I's not so smart, Thomas. (*Check out my Twitter account for more!*)
                                      Tim

...

Dear Tim and/or Eric:
What's the etiquette on telling someone that they are going to make
the biggest mistake of their lives by getting married?
                                        Jessica
                                        Saint George, UT

Dear Jessica:
Make sure you get a prenup.

                                        Eric

                        …

Dear Tim and/or Eric:
"Rainbow Connection" begins with the phrase "Why are there so
many songs about rainbows . . ." but the only song about rainbows
I can think of is "Rainbow Connection." Is this supposed to be irony
or did the frog not do enough research when writing the song?
                                        Liam MacNeil
                                        Waterloo, IA

Dear Liam:
Me know not about it. Henson is songwriters. Might be
with him. Frog is just puppet for him. (*I'm on the Net if you*
want to search for me!)

                                        Tim

                        …

Dear Tim and/or Eric:
I think I might be unconsciously racist. An example: when I walk
down the street and two-plus Mexicans and/or African Americans
are walking toward me, I cross to the other side of the street. Or if

they come into my store, I keep an extra-keen eye on them vs. my nonethnic customers. How do I stop being unconsciously racist?
                                                    Tom from Queens

Dear Tom:
Embrace it. Get an ironic RACIST T-shirt.
                                                    Eric

                                    . . .

Dear Tim and/or Eric:
Sometimes people say "vague-n" instead of "vegan" to be funny and I wonder, is that really funny? Or do you think vegans actually are vague?

                                                    D. Gonzalez
                                                    Los Angeles, CA

Dear D.:
I don't play in those circles. That sound like a scene from a star trick show! Who's pulling my legs with these silly question? (*I have some tracks on iTunes! Surch for me by names!*)
                                                    Tim

                                    . . .

Dear Tim and/or Eric:
Left or right?

                                                    Todd
                                                    Oak Park, IL

Dear Todd:
Right. Or as we like to call it, "Reginald."
                                                    Eric

...

Dear Tim and/or Eric:
I'm ready to pick a new religion. Which do you recommend?
                    Harold Dagis
                    New York, NY

Dear Harold:
I was baptized a Catholic. It has a wonderful American heritage and has a Pope who guides us in our decisions. There is also a liturgy. Thanks for the serious question. (*Chat live with my pastor! I'll give you his screen name!*)
                    Tim

...

Dear Tim and/or Eric:
Do you think the accordion is poised for a comeback?
                    Abigail
                    Vallejo, CA

Dear Abigail:
It never left. Check out Weird Al.
                    Eric

...

Dear Tim and/or Eric:
A burrito is a delicious food item that breaks down all social barriers and leads to temporary spiritual enlightenment. But it is also the Spanish word for "young donkey." Usually there is some kind of

resemblance or shared essence among items that share the same name.
Do you think young donkeys remind people of stuffed tortillas?
Just "Frank"
Wichita, KS

Dear "Frank":
This is another silly questions! What the heck? All this burrito talk is making me hungry though. Not too hot. I don't
like spicy foods. (*Check me out on classmates.com!*)
Tim

. . .

Dear Tim and/or Eric:
It has come to our attention that some of our readers may not "get"
your sense of humor. Even we have to admit that, after reading your
last few responses, it appears that Tim was either stoned or drunk,
and Eric wasn't trying at all. Is this some kind of hipster, postmod-
ern, funny-'cause-it's-not-in-any-way-funny type of thing?
Thank you for your time.
The Believer *magazine*
San Francisco, CA

Dear *The Believer*:
Emanuel, my personal assistant, answered these stimulating
questions. He's new to the English language, so there's a language barrier we all have to deal with at the office. Please
enjoy.

Dictated but not read.
Eric Wareheim

Ed Helms

Dear Ed:
My life partner recently told me that Santa Claus is a homophobe.
Is he right? Santa doesn't seem like the kind of guy who'd be pur-
posefully exclusionary. And that suit, with all the bells and fur
trim, seems a little queeny to me. Maybe my boyfriend just isn't into
fatties?

Callahan N.
Richmond, VA

Dear Callahan:
Your life partner's observation would seem to corroborate my
long-standing assertion that Santa Claus is in fact Rush Lim-
baugh. A brief review of the evidence is both overwhelming
and disturbing. For starters, they both like to chortle. Coin-
cidence? I think not. Second, they both live in an imaginary
universe in which they can say and do positively ridiculous

things with the support and adulation of millions. And finally, they are both undeniably jolly! I'm sorry, Callahan, but it's time you knew the truth about Santa Claus.

Ed

. . .

Dear Ed:
Sometimes I forget to start with the little fork and go straight to the big fork. Is this a problem?

Name withheld
Rockford, IL

Dear Name:
This is a really good question and I hear it all the time. The answer is very simple. If you're genuinely confused about which fork to use, as you clearly are, then you should take the little fork and stab yourself in the left eye. Then take the larger fork and stab yourself in the right eye. At this point you will be in a phenomenal amount of agony and you will be wondering if you will ever see another sunset again. Only then will you truly be free from the tyranny of fork-size equivocation.

Ed

. . .

Dear Ed:
I can't seem to have a restful night's sleep these days, no matter how much booze I drink. What am I doing wrong?!

Jayson Rodgers
Baton Rouge, LA

Dear Jayson:

Your question is fundamentally flawed because it is avoiding the main issue. You have a serious problem. You are addicted to sleep. How many times have you blacked out while sleeping? And I'm willing to bet that when you are sleeping your entire personality changes: you are antisocial and not fun to be around. I don't know you, but I would guess that sleep has begun interfering with your work and your relationships. These are warning signs. Clearly you love booze, which is wonderful, but your addiction to sleep is cutting in on the quality time you get to spend with alcohol. You need to stop sleeping altogether. For this I recommend cocaine.

Ed

...

Dear Ed:

The word "unicorn" always makes me wonder: Why isn't it "uni-horn"? When I hear "unicorn," I think that maybe somebody called it that because they thought the horn looked like a giant corn on the cob and so they just screamed out, "ONE CORN!" which evolved into "unicorn" . . . which makes me think that maybe unicorns are native to Iowa.

Ava
Sioux City, IA

Dear Ava:

Wow. You are really dumb. "Corn" is Latin for "horn," as in "cornucopia." Since Latin is the preferred language for all fauna nomenclature, both real and imaginary, a mono-horned horse is naturally called a unicorn. If anything, you should be asking why corn is named after the Latin word for "horn"! Jeez Louise!

Ed

...

Dear Ed:
I live in a rural part of Texas, and I'm almost positive I saw a Big-
foot. A few times, actually. How do I let him (it?) know that I'm
friendly and mean him no harm? Should I leave some milk and
snacks on my front porch? What do Bigfoots eat anyway?
                                        L.D.
                                        Shreveport, TX

Dear L.D.:
Bigfoots sustain themselves on a strict diet of wild Fijian alba-
core sashimi with pea tendril salad, glazed couscous, asparagus
tips, and red wine jus. Unfortunately, no human can prepare
that dish to the exacting standards of a wild Bigfoot. That
said, they have a less discerning sweet tooth. Try setting out
some praline chicory coffee soufflé, coffee anglaise, and warm
beignets. Just be careful because if the soufflé collapses, the
Bigfoot will get very angry and might try to rape you.
                                        Ed

...

Dear Ed:
I'm pretty sure I saw a giant painting of Kim Jong Il in an upscale
creperie a few weeks ago. What are your thoughts on this combina-
tion (Kim Jong Il and crepes)?
                                        Anthony
                                        Pensacola, FL

Dear Anthony:
It's a little-known fact that Kim Jong Il, despite being a
crazed, megalomaniacal despot, is one of the greatest crepe
chefs in the world. You'll find large portraits and even

shrines to Kim Jong Il in creperies throughout the world. He has contributed immeasurably to the crepe-making oeuvre, perhaps most notably in his daring use of parsley and pine resin. Rumors abound about disturbing human rights violations in some of his crepe-testing laboratories, and his use of forced labor in crepe kitchens is well documented. However, no one can deny the dizzying lightness and delectable nuance of a Kim Jong Il–prepared lemon crêpe suzette.

Ed

…

Dear Ed:
I've always heard that it's not appropriate to wear white after Labor Day, but I never understood why. Is this reverse racism? What's wrong with a little white clothing, as long as there aren't any hoods involved?

Cooper
Sacramento, CA

Hi Cooper:
I recommend never wearing white after Labor Day, mainly because if you do I will murder you. Why? Because I want to cook your organs and eat them so that you will always be a part of me. This may sound weird, but it is rooted in a deep, abiding love for you. That said, I also understand that you may not want to be murdered, and that's why I'm giving you the heads-up. Just know that it really doesn't matter what color your clothes are. I'm probably going to murder you anyway.

Ed

…

Dear Ed:

I really, really want to be famous, but I don't have any talents. Acting, literary, or otherwise. I'm not even all that attractive. Now: How do I get famous?

Christopher
St. Paul, MN

Dear Christopher:

I admire your moxie and determination! It is clear from your letter that you already possess all of the necessary requirements to become famous. In particular, I would encourage you to cultivate your lack of talent, since that has clearly worked well for numerous celebrities. In addition, fame can often be obtained through association. To wit, try hanging out in nightclubs with people who are already famous, like Lindsay Lohan or Dick Cheney. Or might I suggest trouncing Rafael Nadal in the finals at Wimbledon. However you go about it, I wish you good luck and godspeed in your worthy and noble quest!

Ed

Buck Henry

Dear Buck:

Here's what I remember: I started watching a kung fu movie marathon in college, and the next thing I knew I was thirty-four and unemployed. Should I try to figure out what happened to that lost time, or just cut my losses and get on with my life?

Regards,
A Dude in Atlanta, GA

Dear Dude in Atlanta:

That's what you think you remember. We will probably never know what really happened. There is creditable scientific and medical proof that steady exposure to endless repetition—be it of strobe lights, religious chants, Jody cadence (a military training term with which I am sure you are unfamiliar), the music of Don McLean, or even an evening of reality TV—can cause fainting, hallucinations, petit and grand mal seizures, time and space dislocation, and even that old W. C. Fields favorite, mogo on the gogogo. Kung fu marathons are designed to operate on the human limbic system—the sound effects, human grunting, blazing unnatural colors, dizzying athletic pyrotechnics, and pure silliness were designed (probably by General Yamamoto in the waning days of World War II) to stir the occidental brain into sludge. Even today the sound tracks of more than two thousand movies directed by and starring hundreds of people all named Lee are played day and night in the Guantánamo prison system as an adjunct to waterboarding. I'd leave your lost past alone if I were you. You might have been al Qaeda.

Cheers,
Buck

...

Dear Buck:
I just read Siddhartha *to impress a girl, and I'm having trouble thinking of anything to say about it that would sound sufficiently deep but not too pretentious. Any ideas?*
Thanks,
Joshua
Chicago, IL

Dear Joshua:
Be careful. A woman who would actually request that someone she ostensibly cares for should read *Siddhartha* is intellectually ruthless if not criminally insane. This is a trap. You must realize by now that there is nothing that you or anyone else can say about Hesse's novel without seeming pretentious or, even worse, foreign. When I was very young, my great-grandmother, who was old and ill, asked me to read her to

sleep. I selected *Siddhartha* because I surmised that I was in her will. She passed away during chapter two. I was amazed that she lasted that long.

Buck

...

Dear Buck:

My husband only has one testicle. I try not to make him feel bad about it—his other ball was removed after doctors discovered it was cancerous—but every time I look at his groin, I think, Hitler only had one testicle, too. Is that terrible of me? My husband is a good man, and despite the unfortunate physical similarities, he has nothing else in common with one of the worst hatemongers in history.

Susan P.

Omaha, NE

Dear Susan P:

Heinrich Himmler, who was not only a Nazi butcher but also a famous ass-kisser, once said to Hitler: "Mein Führer, some men may see your scrotum as half-empty; I see it as half-full." Susan, there are many men who are unitesticular, and it doesn't mean that they're anti-Semitic or about to invade Poland. One of our most famous bodybuilding strongmen (not, I assure you, our beloved California governor) was reputed to be gonadically challenged, and he has many friends of the Hebrew persuasion who find him to be socially charming and mildly threatening only when faced with scary deli food. Your problem, such as it is, puts me in mind of my favorite burlesque sketch, which I saw as a youth in Jersey City. Maybe you will think of this the next time you are staring at your husband's sole orb of regeneration and chuckle instead of recoil. A married couple make their first visit to a nudist colony. In their cabin, the husband looks out the window and says: "My god, I'm not going out there with all those crazy people." And the wife says: "Why are you calling them crazy?" And he answers: "Well, can't you see their nuts?" I'm still laughing.

Buck

. . .

Dear Buck:

I've been dating this guy for a few weeks and I think I really like him. But he's in a wheelchair. When and if we finally have sex, what can I expect? Does he have to stay in the chair the whole time? And if not, can he be on top?

Cheers,

N.D.

Holyoke, MA

Dear N.D.:

Wheelchair sex is not as complicated as it might seem, but it can be dangerous. Its customs and general usages go as far back as the Kama Sutra, which contains the first, and perhaps the only, recorded case of how to make love when one of the lovers is basically attached to a form of conveyance. I am too refined to give you the full details, but this moving tale involves a love-smitten gal from Calcutta and the object of her affection, a young prince who, because of a skating accident, was confined to an elephant. Need I say more?

Buck

. . .

Dear Buck:
At what age is quitting your job and becoming a full-time carnie no longer socially acceptable?

> *Best,*
> *Eric*
> *Augusta, ME*

Dear Eric:
Quitting your boring and meaningless daily grind for the life of the open road and a close if not intimate relationship with really angry wild animals and lovable clowns who wear funny disguises to protect themselves from being pointed out by children in the audience whom they have touched inappropriately (if not killed and eaten) can never be considered a socially unacceptable choice. It is at the very least adventurous, and at worst suicidal. We are in an uncertain economy. But there will always be openings in the carnie for a powerful roustabout or—and I suspect this is more up your alley—a really hungry geek.

> Buck

Mindy Kaling

Dear Mindy:
I read somewhere that dolphins are the only animals (besides humans) who engage in gang rape. Is that true? And if it is, should I remove the dolphin posters from my daughter's bedroom walls?
Sincerely,
D. Sachs
Pittsburgh, PA

Dear D.:
I am facing a similar situation. My teenage son fancies himself an artist. To that end, he has hung up a very unsettling print by M. C. Escher on his wall. There's just something about a hand drawing itself that I find unsavory. But you

have given me a great idea. I am going to tell my son that
M. C. Escher was a rapist.

> Thanks,
> Mindy

...

Dear Mindy:

*I recently discovered that my fiancé is a cat burglar. I have no prob-
lem dating a criminal, but does he have to use such ridiculous 1950s
terminology? I imagine him going to work dressed in a black turtle-
neck and an eye mask and a bag with a big dollar sign written on
the side flung over his shoulders. How should I tell him that I'm
losing all respect for him?*

> *Katie L.*
> *Grand Rapids, MI*

Dear Katie,
I'm sorry, but I stopped reading after I read the word
"fiancé." Lady, what are you trying to prove? Does the word
"fiancé" need to be used, ever? "Boyfriend" or "serious
boyfriend" suffices just fine. People who drop French words
like "fiancé" or "joie de vivre" are the real criminals, not your
interesting-sounding boyfriend.

> Mindy

...

Dear Mindy:

*My husband is a terrible author. He's been working on the same
novel for almost a decade, and I'm so tired of reading his "latest
revision." I just can't fake it anymore, and he gets suspicious when I*

claim to have a headache or eye cramps. How can I avoid his sloppy prose while also sparing his feelings?

Guilty Wife in Baton Rouge

Dear Guilty Wife:
You think the fact that he's bad is the reason you hate reading his stuff, but it's not. When I carried on my decades-long affair with Tom Wolfe—you should've seen the two of us, nattily dressed in matching white suits—he always asked me to read his work. It was dreadful. It got to the point where I had to put down chapter two of *The Right Stuff* and say: "They go to space, they don't go to space, I don't care anymore!" And he's a good writer. It's torture. I would check into a women's shelter.

Regards,
Mindy

. . .

Dear Mindy:
I've been living with my boyfriend for eight years and my family still thinks he's my roommate. I don't know how to be any more obvious. We sleep in the same bed, for god's sake. Do I have to give him oral sex in front of them before they get it?

Brad
Sioux Falls, SD

Dear Brad:
Are you acting recognizably gay? Are you a flamboyant emotional wreck like Nathan Lane in *The Birdcage*? Or petulant and *muy caliente* like Hank Azaria in *The Birdcage*? Or are you basically a swarthy straight man, but gay, like Robin Williams in *The Birdcage*? Emulate these iconic gay fixtures. "Gayge" (wordplay) your gayness, and then just kick it up a

notch (Emeril). Everyone loves this movie and your parents will soon get the picture.

Best,
Mindy

. . .

Dear Mindy:

My bass player wants to break up the band because we're all turn-ing forty next month and he thinks it's not awesome to be playing Cheap Trick covers when you're forty. How can I tell him he's wrong, so wrong?

Still Awesome in Cleveland, OH

Dear Still Awesome:

In Donald Justice's famous poem "Men at Forty," he talks about this very phenomenon. I don't remember it word for word, but I believe what he says is that your friend closes doors softly now, and also that he probably wants to stop playing with your band because he's bent on killing himself, and he wants to be alienated from as many people as possible prior to the act. If it sounds like a kick-ass poem, that's cuz it totally is.

Mindy

. . .

Dear Mindy:

I've told my mistress that I intend to leave my wife eventually and run away with her. But she has to understand that I have no inten-tion of doing anything of the kind, right? I mean, anybody who has been on this planet for longer than a month knows that cheaters don't mean anything they say. If we did, we wouldn't be cheaters.

But somehow I don't think she gets the implied and unspoken agreement of an extramarital affair. What should I do?
            Warmly,
            S.H.
            Westfield, MA

Dear S.H.:

Dude, you totally have to kill her. I only have a cursory understanding of this type of situation, but I've seen movies like *Match Point* and *I Am Legend* and I know how hard it can be to be in an adulterous relationship, and I also know a man can live alone for, like, years and years, if you store food and only go out during daylight. Kill her!

            Cheers,
            Mindy

Thomas Lennon

Dear Thomas:
My wife asked me not to curse around our kids, but I think it's healthy for them to become well versed in swear words. Isn't the freedom to call somebody a "cocksucking motherfucker" a constitutional right, even for an eight-year-old boy? Maybe what he needs isn't less cursing, but more creative cursing?

> *Jim B.*
> *Burlingame, CA*

Dear Jim:
Your son is going to learn about cocksucking either at home or behind Arby's. If your wife continues to violate your constitutional rights, sue her. I do, however, agree that more creative cursing could broaden the boy's horizons. Try new curses like "fuckwinch" or "assgratch." If the boy picks up some of these words, he could become the next Faulkner,

or just some crazy-ass motherfucker sucking cock behind Arby's.

Tom

...

Dear Thomas:
My friend told me to skip community college because the drugs aren't as good and therefore the education isn't as good. Is that true? Is a university only as intellectually stimulating as its drug supply?
Eric Schmidt
Charlotte, NC

Dear Eric:
This is entirely true. You should seriously consider a college in Amsterdam, where the magic mushrooms can be purchased both legally and in either the dried or fresh variety. The classes will be in Dutch, but it won't matter, because you'll be tripping your balls off.

Tom

...

Dear Thomas:
I got my ears pierced in high school. I got my first nose piercing in college. After graduation, I got my tongue pierced. A few weeks ago, I got my nipples pierced. Given the geographical direction of my piercings, is it only a matter of time before there's a steel stud in my testicles?
"Holes" Thomsen
St. Louis, MO

Dear "Holes":
Bravo, sir! Yes, a steel post through the fleshy sac of your manhood looms on the horizon. But take note: your body

should reflect the ideal feng shui bagua. That means: metal left earring for creativity/children, wooden right earring for family/foundation, something shoved through your nose that's on fire for fame/reputation, and a jug of water hanging from your ball post for career/life path.

Tom

...

Dear Thomas:
Will you settle a bet between my friend and me? He says that PoMo is shorthand for postmodern. I think it's a deli sandwich that's sometimes served with capicola and provolone cheese. Who's right?

Sam Hittleman
Traverse City, MI

Dear Sam:
You're both wrong. PoMo is either Brazilian surfer slang for "a Portuguese man-of-war" or DC slang for "a poor mosh pit." For example: "That's a PoMo, especially for a Fugazi show." A capicola/provolone sandwich is called a Coppola.

Tom

...

Dear Thomas:
I want to get lipo and have the fat sucked out of my fat fucking thighs. But my boyfriend says I should save the money and use it to buy more books. Isn't he just pulling my fat leg? What is more attractive—a well-read fattie or a stick figure who can't spell her own name?

Confused (and fat)
Kansas City, KS

Dear Confused (and fat):

Bless you for thinking that men might like a well-read woman. We're actually attracted to both stick figures and massive hoggies, but none of us particularly care about your reading habits, unless you're reading books about how to give better blow jobs.

My advice is: skip the books and the lipo and invest in a good pair of Spanx panty hose. It'll create the illusion of toned, muscular thighs.

Cheers,
Tom

Al Madrigal

Dear Al:
I'm completely broke and considering either donating my eggs or a career as an escort. Both of these sound like a good way for a girl to get cash quickly and easily. Which do you recommend?
Hottie with Great SAT Scores
New York, NY

Dear Hottie:
Look, I loved *Pretty Woman* as much as any straight male possibly could, but let's be realistic. A Richard Gere type is going to come along at best once a year. Most of your average "clients" trolling for hookers are literally guys who *have to pay for sex*. That means a lot of physical deformities and dickheads. So, not only are you gonna see more than your fair share of eye patches and jaw-dropping eczema, you're gonna get slapped by a lot worse than Jason Alexander.

By the way, a prosthetic hand hurts way worse than a real one. So let's support the culture of life and help create it instead of almost losing it three times a day.

Al

...

Dear Al:
I hate all the chemicals they put into bug repellents. Can you recommend a natural alternative?

Itchy in Oregon

Dear Itchy:
Short of buying a hundred magnifying glasses and burning every bug in sight, why don't you shut up and embrace science, you dirty hippie? DEET, like TV and the Internet, is good. The next time you want to go *Into the Wild* with a bag of flaxseeds and a dream catcher to tap into your inner Earth Mother, remember we didn't cure polio with a drum circle and some patchouli oil.

Al

...

Dear Al:
Is a homemade tie-dyed T-shirt ever a good idea for somebody who uses deodorant and doesn't enjoy jam bands?

Dana in Jupiter, FL

Dear Dana:
Yes. But be careful, a tie-dyed shirt is gateway fashion. Without the proper level of awareness, a tie-dyed shirt can lead to Teva sandals and Guatemalan print shorts.

Al

...

Dear Al:
I may be going to jail soon and I'm just curious, is it more like the
TV show Oz *or the TV show* Hogan's Heroes*? Or does it depend*
on the state? I just want to know what to expect.
                    Randell
                    Lubbock, TX

Dear Randell:

If you're writing in to *The Believer* to ask this question, I
would assume you're not prison material. In fact it's probably a good bet that you are writing this looking through
horn-rimmed glasses while wearing a pair of skinny jeans. So
when it comes to prison you can hope for *Hogan's Heroes*, but
you need to plan for *American Me*. Because, while we'd all
like to think that lockup involves old men tending birds,
whittling, hard-boiled-egg eating contests, and converting
to new and exciting religions, it's important for you to be
realistic. Know this: you're going to be assaulted physically,
verbally, and mentally twenty-four seven. Good luck, and
BTW, there is no shame in suicide.

                    Al

...

Dear Al:
For most of my life, I solved the majority of my problems by asking,
"What would Jesus do?" But now I'm stumped. What do you sup-
pose would be Jesus' opinion of saddlebagging?
                    Frank O.
                    Asheville, NC

Dear Frank:

I am quite proud to admit that I don't know what saddle-bagging is, and I refuse to Google it. But we can assume that any act so depraved or ridiculous that it has to be given a cute nickname is more or less disgusting. While I'm not the most religious guy, even discussing the Judeo-Christian Lord and saddlebagging at the same time makes me a little bit uncomfortable.

Al

Aasif Mandvi

Dear Aasif:
I have a problem. My boyfriend borrowed my cat for a slumber party
and is now refusing to return him. It's been over a month. I go there
enough that it's not really a big deal, but I miss owning this ani-
mal. How can I make the cat come back without having a violent
domestic dispute?

Lumpy's owner
Providence, RI

Dear Lumpy's owner:
Why on earth would you let your boyfriend borrow your cat
for a slumber party? Does this even make sense to you? I can
tell you why the cat will never return to you. The cat has been
exposed to homoeroticism, and having now been exposed to
this lifestyle with a group of young teenage boys, he is likely
unable to return to your home and live a normal life.

The boyfriend is not keeping the cat hostage. What has happened is this cat, now addicted to the sweet nectar of homo-deviant sexual behavior, is now unable to reenter society. I would say you shouldn't visit your cat, because it will only bring heartache. As the cat's need for more and more stimulating sexual adventures increases, you may find that he begins to peruse gay nightclubs and bars, and soon this could lead to a life of prostitution and drugs. That's right, *drugs.* You need to forget this cat and get yourself a new, wholesome cat that has not been tainted by a wild night of slumber party games that involve prepubescent boys and a stick.

Tough break, kid. Next time someone says, "Hey, can I borrow your cat for a slumber party?" I hope you'll think twice before ruining another feline life.

Aasif

. . .

Dear Aasif:
I have body issues. I think I am a skinny person, but really have gained a considerable amount of weight since 2007. I don't want to buy new clothes and I love to eat.
What do I do?
Fatty Threw a Party and Now Her Jeans Hurt to Wear
Wichita Falls, TX

Dear Fatty:
Nothing. If you think you are a skinny person then *you are.* It's not the outside that matters; it's the inside. How you see yourself in your mind's eye is how others will see you in the real world. If your clothes don't fit you anymore, just act like they do, and guess what? *They will fit you!* If you are fat and want to be thin, then just tell yourself that you are thin. The

greatest diet in the world is the one that takes place in YOUR MIND.

I once met a woman whose pants were so tight around her obviously overweight ass and stomach that her jeans remained completely unbuttoned to the point where the mall security guard had to escort her out of the mall. Do you think this woman accepted the reality of her body? Hell no! Did this woman let the weight win and buy new pants? Hell no! Did this woman say to herself, "I shouldn't go to the mall if I can't button my jeans"? Hell no! Did this woman say, "I am thin and these clothes fit me just fine because reality has nothing to do with what is real"? Hell yes! This is America! Go, girl! You've never looked so good!

Aasif

...

Dear Aasif:
Is it fair to force my dog to be a vegetarian?
Lucie
Asheville, NC

Dear Lucie:
I would suggest that you not "force" your dog to be a vegetarian, because forcing will get you into a power struggle with an animal. And that's always sad to see, because as humans, we have all the money and the guns and the treats. Instead, you should use well-established training methods to teach your dog about the benefits of being a vegetarian.

The key word here is "respect." If you don't respect the fact that your dog comes from a long line of meat eaters, you will not earn his trust, and in the end you won't be able to manipulate his will. Your dog, if he is like other dogs, has probably been told that eating meat is part of the culture of being a dog. This is baloney. The problem is that eating meat is where his canine identity lies, just like chewing on bones and barking and chasing the mailman. All these things are part of his Current Canine Identity (CCI). However, having written an extensive pamphlet on the subject, I can categorically tell you that what's needed is to Reverse His Canine Identity (RHCI). It's been well documented that vegetarian dogs are smarter, less violent, and have fresher breath than their meat-eating counterparts. So, when you catch him chewing on a bone, replace it with a stick of celery. (Paint it brown if you have to.) If he notices and refuses to touch it, just leave the celery in his bowl until it turns into a brown, moldy liquid. Eventually starvation will kick in and voilà, you and your dog will be working together toward a mutual goal. If he barks, let loose a roar that is louder and more intimidating than anything he's ever heard. In my case, with my dachshund, I purchased a cassette tape of a lion roaring from the National Geographic audio library, and I let it play at full volume, sometimes in the middle of the night, very close to his ears while he's sleeping. It creates a nightmare association that's quite effective.

Once these few lessons have been learned, you'll be on your way to having an obedient dog. Because of this method, I have a well-behaved and mostly mute celery-eating dog who whimpers whenever the mailman comes around. Good luck to you, Lucie. For more information and questions you can purchase my pamphlet at veggiedog.co.uk.org/whimper.

Aasif

Marc Maron

Dear Marc:
My mother-in-law hates me, but that's not really my problem. I think I'm developing a crush on her boyfriend. Is that too weird? How soon should I tell my wife about these feelings, if at all? And is there a chance this has something to do with why my mother-in-law hates my guts?

> *Giles Russo*
> *Durham, NC*

Dear Giles:
You've got a lot of things going on here, on a lot of levels. Generally, when family is involved and there is so much unsaid, it is best just to come out with it abruptly and without provocation in the middle of a holiday dinner. It might even be good to offer to say a prayer before the meal and do

a gratitude/confessional thing. The worst that can happen is that the meal turns into a mess of emotional chaos and everyone, for their own reasons, leaves the table and you are left alone eating your last supper as the man you were and your first supper of your new life with the muted sounds of crying and yelling drifting in from other rooms.

Marc

. . .

Dear Marc:

My wife left me for a woman, and though I think I should feel terrible about this, my friends tell me that I shouldn't take it personally. She isn't rejecting me; she's rejecting all *men. I suppose they have a point, but am I wrong to think that I was dumped for reasons that have nothing to do with my penis?*

H. V. Bewley
New York, NY

Dear H. V.:

The sad truth is that she was probably gay going in and you seemed like enough of a lesbian for her to try to snap out of what she hoped was a phase. I say get rid of the penis and try to get her back. You can do that now. I saw it in a special on HBO.

Marc

. . .

Dear Marc:

I've been thinking about leaving the country ever since Bush was reelected, but I can't decide on the right place to go. Canada is too cold, Mexico is too dangerous, nobody likes Americans (even expats)

in France, and Britain seems as oppressive and fascistic as home.
I'm out of ideas! Any suggestions?

Sandy P.
Somewhere in Iowa

Dear Sandy:

Don't be a coward. Fight for your beliefs and your country. If you are that fed up with America, start your own country. If you have a little property and a vision, all you need is a constitution. Write it up, make yourself president, head of the military, chief legislator, and Supreme Court justice. Then create some uniforms that you can wear for each role. Build a Sandyland MySpace page and reach out to like-minded people who might want to become citizens. This is the DIY age, Sandy. Make technology work for you. Oh, and write a snappy national anthem and decide on a few regional tourist attractions to bring in some money. If you have a dog, there's the Sandyland National Zoological Park. You get the idea.

Marc

...

Dear Marc:
My boyfriend makes me talk dirty to him during sex, but I can't think of anything to say that isn't a cliché or doesn't make me sound like a porn star. Can you suggest some conversational topics for sex that are both clever and filthy?

Andrea Gordon
Provo, UT

Dear Andrea:
Talk to him like you're fifteen and having a fight with your father.

Marc

...

Dear Marc:
My wife is pregnant, and though I love her and everything, she's been kind of an asshole lately. I know it's really because of the hormones, but I'm not sure how much more of this I can take. How can I tell her to fuck off in the most polite, I-still-love-you-because-you're-the-mother-of-my-child-but-c'mon-you're-being-a-cunt kinda way?

Jack Caldwell
Chicago, IL

Dear Jack:
Just know that any missteps on your part during this harrowing period of pregnancy will be held against you for the rest of your life. Any action you take along the lines that you are thinking will be seen as selfish, immature, insensitive, and perhaps unforgivable. Be politically minded here. Have a little vision. Think about the future. Your wife feels fat, farty, unattractive, and uncomfortable. Do whatever she wants you to do and make her feel loved and sexy. Meanwhile, nourish your resentment of her. Store it and mold it into an emotional disposition that will make your new child love you more than its mother.

Marc

...

Dear Marc:

I have a weird feeling that Bob Dylan's "Tangled Up in Blue" was written about me. I've never dated, been married to, or even met Mr. Dylan, but some of the details in his song are just too eerily similar to my own life. I've worked in a topless bar for most of my adult life, and I'm fond of reading Italian poetry (yes, from the eighteenth century) to my boyfriend. Also, I don't care for either homemade bread or small bank accounts. Am I just being paranoid, or is Dylan trying to get my attention?

> *Anjanette H.*
> *San Francisco, CA*

Dear Anjanette:

There is no doubt in my mind that you are absolutely correct about your feelings. To get some real clarity, begin a daily crystal meth regimen. Start out slow but do it until hallucinations induced by sleep deprivation become your guide. I think it will be clear that you need to follow Dylan—he's always on the road—and when the time is right, corner him and tell him everything you are thinking. Try to maintain some charm through this process. If your hair and teeth start falling out, you've waited too long to make your move.

> Marc

...

Dear Marc:

After twenty years of marriage, my wife suddenly announced that she wants an open relationship. At first, it felt like I'd won the lottery. But lately it's occurred to me that I'm a fortysomething man with a paunch, and she's a trim hottie in her sexual prime. Am I setting myself up for disaster?

> *Stephen Goldstone*
> *Jacksonville, FL*

Dear Stephen:

It doesn't sound like you have much of a choice. You only have a few options. I don't know how you are set up financially, but you might want to get some Viagra and put an image together that would make younger women think that you are well-off and virile and dupe them into sex that way. Or you could level the playing field by finding a woman your own age, telling her what you've been through, and actually having an age-appropriate relationship. My fear is that you will be left no choice but to unintentionally reveal your fear and desperation to your current wife and tell her she can do whatever she wants as long as you are part of it somehow. Then you spend the rest of your life quietly masturbating in a closet while she fucks a seemingly never-ending parade of men in your bed. The only way this scenario can end is, a day comes when you wrap your lips around the end of a shotgun. On that sad day, I would make sure you are in the closet and she is in the middle of a particularly heated fuck session when that hammer comes down.

Come on, Stephen. Open relationship? Are you out of your fucking mind? Lose her.

Marc

Adam McKay

Dear Adam:
I've heard that you can legally buy marijuana if you have glau-
coma. I'd like to avoid optic nerve damage, as anything on or around
my eyes kinda creeps me out. Are there non-eyeball diseases that
would allow me to smoke government-sanctioned weed?
                                        Thanks,
                                        Sandy
                                        San Francisco, CA

Dear Sandy:
You've asked a very intriguing question. Right now, in the
great state of California, there are many ailments that doctors
will treat with weed: back pain, anxiety, that time of the
month, etc., etc. Some lesser-known ailments include: being
bitten by a fruit bat (let's face it, if you've been bitten by a
poodle-size bat, you need to get high fast so you can laugh

about it), being dead (8 percent of marijuana users are zombies, thus explaining their slow walk and lack of jobs), and being haunted by a ghost (if you walk into a doctor's office and yell, "The ghosts won't get out of my head!" what serious professional won't hook you up with some ganja immediately?).

Adam

. . .

Dear Adam:
I've heard so much recently about an impending global grain shortage. Should I be hoarding bread?

John B.
Seattle, WA

Dear John:
It's shocking to me that you haven't already been hoarding bread. I'm going to assume you're Amish and don't have access to any kind of useful information. I started hoarding bread back in '79 and now have approximately thirty-four tons of fermented bread in U-Store-Its across the country. I've got Wonder bread with Justice League of America trading cards in it, and frozen Lender's bagels from '82. Recently I was arrested for operating a still because apparently the guards at the storage facilities were getting drunk off of my old bread. But that's a problem I can live with, while you starve to death up there in Washington State.

Adam

. . .

Dear Adam:
According to the old adage, "Beer before liquor, never been sicker; liquor before beer, you're in the clear." But what if you prefer

*popping bennies? Where's the snappy, helpful rhyme for those of us
who like our bliss in pill form?*

T.J.
Portland, OR

Dear T.J.:
It's tough to be from the Northwest, because popular culture
and medicine take decades to get to you folks. Having said
that, we Easterners and Southwesterners thank you for your
gold and potatoes. The saying is "Bennies before Dilaudid,
never clouded; huffing Wite-Out before injecting CAT into
your dick, you might get a smidge sick." Another popular
one in my neck of the woods is "Grain alcohol before a glass
of liquid acid, always placid; pulling a three-hundred-dude
train while high on angel dust before cliff diving on meth
will lead to televised death." A good way to remember these
is to put them to a popular song melody. I use Rage Against
the Machine's cover of "Maggie's Farm." Hope I was able to
help! And when you guys get phone lines out there in Oregon, give us a call and let us know how it worked!

Adam

...

Dear Adam:
*I'm not a virgin, but every time I have sex with a woman, I tell her,
"This is my first time." It gives her a sense of accomplishment, and
my below-average skills in the bedroom suddenly seem really
impressive. Am I being immoral, or just making lemonade out of
lemons?*

Not a Virgin but Willing to Learn
Ann Arbor, MI

Dear Not a Virgin:

Lies and fantasy are the nectar of good lovemaking. What you're doing is adding spice to both your lives, and spice is never bad, unless it's condensed into a highly concentrated form and put into a spray can and sprayed at a person's eyes. I myself will sometimes tell a lover I was raised in the Koresh compound and was taught that sex with more than one girl is wrong and I will burst into flame if it happens and that's why girls won't do it. After she brings her crying friend into the room to join us, the fun begins. So if it makes you feel good, it can't be wrong. Which is why I'm addicted to cooking sherry, glory-hole sex, and blackjack.

Adam

...

Dear Adam:

I really want my vote to count in the upcoming election, but I'm confused. Would you help me make sense of the Democratic and Republican candidates? I just need something short and snappy and easy to understand so I can go get drunk with my buds and stop worrying about the world.

Chad (please no "hanging" jokes please)
Boston, MA

Dear Hanging Chad:

Politics are tough. That's why I will ask my teenage daughter who she thinks is cuter. This year she said Zach from *Zach & Cody*, so he's getting my vote. I love democracy!

Adam

Eugene Mirman

Dear Eugene:
Can you settle a bet for me? I say that it's okay to load the dish-
washer with different-size plates next to each other, but my mom says
that I'll never find my own apartment or produce grandchildren. My
driving privileges are on the line—which one of us is right?
                                        Thanks,
                                        Perry in Peril
                                        Parker, CO

Dear Perry in Peril:
What you have asked is technically a "non-question," because
the very notion of doing dishes is flawed. When possible,
dishes should be tossed out a window. I know my answer
isn't very "green," but the time saved will let you make a
much bigger impact in your community.

   On a separate issue, if your mother has told you that

grandchildren are in some way produced by using a dish-washer, she is lying.

Take care,
Eugene

...

Dear Eugene:
I drive a 1997 Honda Civic with 178,000 miles on it. Lately, it's been making an odd noise and vibrating wildly whenever I apply the brakes at highway speeds. Because the car is stolen, I'm reluctant to take it to an authorized mechanic. Does this sound like a serious problem, or can I afford to ignore it for a while?

Cheers,
Dave
Wilmington, DE

Dear Dave:
It sounds like something is wrong with your transmission. You need to get it checked out right away. How am I so sure even though I've never owned a car? Because I own something a little more useful than knowledge—I own confidence. Go to the mechanic. Be careful, though. If the mechanic calls the police, you'll have only about ten minutes to run away. How will you know if he's called the police? He'll try to stall you with questions and tasks like, "Want to write a play with me right now?" "Let's watch the movie *Dune*," or, "How do the pieces in chess move again?" It'll be obvious.

Eugene

...

Dear Eugene:
My sister has always had a real zest for life, but lately I've noticed that she seems to be drinking more than usual. I'm also not thrilled with the guys she's been "dating." How can I approach her about this without sounding like an uptight, repressed spinster?

> *All the best,*
> *Prudence*
> *Schenectady, NY*

Dear Prudence:
First of all, thank you for giving me the opportunity to write "Dear Prudence." It was really fun.

You have the age-old problem of a slightly drunk sister throwing her body a party and inviting, indiscriminately, guys she met at a flea market and several bassists. Often people have to realize on their own that they're making mistakes. (Robert Downey, Jr., and Amy Winehouse are just two examples.) Still, you can accelerate the process. Fill your sister's pillow with thousands of pieces of paper that say "You're making a mistake," and, "You need to cut down on drinking." When she brings some dude home, they'll lie down and be like, "These pillows feel weird." Once they look inside and find all the notes, they'll be like, "Your sister really loves you. We shouldn't be doing this."

You can also handcuff her to a golden retriever. I don't know if you've ever tried drinking or making out while handcuffed to a dog, but I bet it's near impossible.

> Eugene

. . .

Dear Eugene:
I'm a middle school student and I'm not very athletic. This is a problem because most of the other kids are, and they always play

basketball together at recess. I want to play, too, but I'm afraid I won't be good enough. What if they laugh at me for the rest of the year?

> *Regards,*
> *Ball's in My Court*
> *Myrtle Beach, SC*

Dear Ball's in My Court:

Oh my god! You are afraid of the wrong thing! What if they laugh at you for the *rest of the year*? No, that's not what you should worry about. What if they laugh at you for the next five years? What happens if that leads you to never believe in yourself? What if you seek solace in drugs or, worse, community theater? You can't allow that to happen. You have to overcome your fear of being laughed at and develop an insurmountable self-confidence. How? Not by turning to whiskey—that's what weak tweens do, and you're strong. You need a three-pronged approach:

1. Start playing basketball somewhere alone for two hours a day for at least one day, but more like a month.

2. Pick two other things to become not just good at, but great at. A few options: backgammon, karate, computers, or premarital sex. (JK—don't do it.)

3. Absorb the following knowledge: sports are one of the most important things at your age, but they exponentially decrease in importance after high school—just ask Mick Jagger or Janet Reno—plus at around twenty-eight everyone becomes overweight and sluggish, and the most important things become happiness, money, and having (or being) a pretty wife who smiles really well (and doesn't let on that everything is awful).

> Eugene

. . .

Dear Eugene:
My friend Andrew is experiencing a renaissance after a relative
nadir in his love life. I want to buy him a gift that says, "Yeah,
dude. You're doing it. Be safe." What would you suggest?
                    Sandy
                    San Francisco, CA

P.S. He is a box turtle.

Dear Sandy:
Well, obviously you don't need to get him condoms or anything like that. My guess is he already has an iPod. You
should build him a turtle-size modern home with glass
walls, a steam shower, hot tub, and lettuce room—basically
Howard Roark the place. A classy turtle is a happy turtle.
                    Eugene

P.S. If the reason your friend is experiencing a renaissance in
his love life is because you bought another turtle and put her
in his cage, then you are no better than Indian parents who
make their daughter marry some rich family's son in exchange
for horses and weird drums. I know, why end this with a confused, ethnically charged remark? So you start seeing turtles
like I do—as pawns in a cultural war.

Morgan Murphy

Dear Morgan:
My boyfriend wants to go to Burning Man, but the last time he was
there, he had sex with a man covered in silver body paint. He says
it was just a onetime thing—how often do you get to fuck a silver
man?—but I'm worried that it might happen again. Am I right to
be concerned?

> *Glenn*
> *Davenport, IA*

Dear Glenn:
I hate to break it to you, but your boyfriend is gaaaaay. You
two fellas have obviously been together awhile if this is his
second Burning Man, but if he's fucking a man (covered in
silver paint, no less), then he is a homosexual, and you need
to figure out if that's something you're willing to live with.
I would advise approaching him gently on this subject, as

nobody wants to be dragged out of the closet. Perhaps bring it up to him while he's blowing you.

Above all, don't judge him. I happen to know that you're required to fuck a man covered in silver paint to get into Burning Man. It's a policy established in 1998, after a complaint that paper tickets were wasteful and added to the festival's already excessive littering. Inserting one's penis into a silver man is the ultimate form of recycling. That way, if the Burning Man Police want to know if you've paid your entrance fee, they can simply ask to see your silver penis. It's quite brilliant in its simplicity, and kind to Mother Earth. Other events now implementing the "fuck a man covered in silver body paint" policy include Lollapalooza, various FM radio stations' "Jingle Balls," and the Westminster Dog Show.

Morgan

...

Dear Morgan:
I've read that by drinking one and a half glasses of red wine each day, you can prevent cancer and heart attacks. My question is, what happens if you finish the second glass? Are you undoing all the good?
Sandra Olston
Orlando, FL

Dear Sandra:
Allow me to ask you a question, Sandra. Why would you want to prevent cancer and heart attacks? Do you have any idea how nice people are to you when you've recently been diagnosed with lymphoma, or undergone a coronary bypass? I've endured three years of white-knuckled, unassisted sobriety in the hopes that I might be stricken down by a temporarily debilitating illness that will force God-fearing family members to wait on me hand and foot. Sure, when I

see my friends going to Party Town (choo choo!) with a case of Shiraz, part of me wants to join them. But then I think about said friends having to bathe me with sponges during my bedridden "vacation" from life's responsibilities. Why would I want to prevent that? People say "fed through a tube" like it's a bad thing. I see it as a simplified alternative to the ever cumbersome fork and spoon. And don't even get me started on chopsticks.

Morgan

. . .

Dear Morgan:
I love James Patterson thrillers, but whenever my friends catch me reading one of his books, they give me a look like it's Gang Bang Trannies. *Should I give up on my guilty pleasure and choke down more Don DeLillo and Thomas Pynchon, or get less judgmental friends?*

Leo P.
Richton Park, IL

Dear Leo:
I can't believe you would make up such a convoluted story just so you could reference Thomas Pynchon and Don DeLillo in the same sentence. Nice work, douche bag.

I am also personally insulted by your mockery of *Gang Bang Trannies*. I'll have you know that it's the greatest fictional depiction of polyamory since *Little Women II*, Louisa May Alcott's harrowing follow-up about four lesbian midgets who fuck one another in post–Civil War New England.

Why would you write to a magazine and ask a question about books? Do you think I'd write a letter to *The Five People You Meet in Heaven* asking Mitch Albom if I should continue to read *XXL*? Actually, that's a poor example. Have you read *Tuesdays with Morrie*? That guy could answer anything. Now that I think about it, you should probably try to get his advice.

Morgan

...

Dear Morgan:
Is it wrong to have sex with somebody I respect but don't find physically attractive? I've been dating this guy for a few weeks, and while the sex has been repulsive, our postcoital conversations are always stimulating and fulfilling. Is there something wrong with me?

Jenny Godfrey
Rapid City, SD

Dear Jenny:
Allow me to answer your last question first. Yes, there is something wrong with you. You're retarded. I don't mean retarded in the casual sense (i.e., "You're retarded"). I am clinically diagnosing you as a person with mental retardation. Because you are retarded, I don't expect you to understand the difference, but trust me when I say that my use of the word "retarded" is not offensive at all. Sex repulses you not because your boyfriend is unattractive, but because you have the mind of a seven-year-old. Your postcoital conversations (no idea how you whipped out that word, but I once saw a retarded person on *Live with Regis and Kelly* who could count backward, so I'll believe just about anything) are stimulating because who doesn't enjoy a conversation with a man who has sex with retarded girls? Now that's a guy with stories!

Morgan

Bob Odenkirk

Dear Bob:
I have romantic intentions toward an incredibly hot boy who lives in
my dorm, but my friends tell me not to bother, because he's out of my
league. How do they know that? Isn't beauty subjective?
                    Thanks,
                    Pretty Confident in Her Own Attractiveness
                    Hartford, CT

Dear PCIHOA:
Your acronym-name is worthless. Do better on that next
time. I'm very tired. Got the kids off to school this morning,
forgot to put water, vegetable, or sandwich in son's lunch
bag, just filled it with napkins. Have you seen Larry King
lately? He's thinner, bonier, and hotter than ever. What's
with the Olympic torch? It's silly. The Olympics are silly.
Clowns, too. Have you ever eaten pie? Do. You'll thank me.

Does that answer your question? No? I say ask the guy out. Beauty is subjective and he sounds like a great guy to me, the kind who might enjoy a pinch-faced, watery-eyed, drooling boob such as yourself. Hope that helps.

Best,

Bob

. . .

Dear Bob:

What's the proper way to refrigerate venison? I've tried storing the carcass in my basement freezer, but it always ends up with a gamey taste. What am I doing wrong?

Too Much Deer Meat

Suttons Bay, MI

Dear TMDM:

Your acronym-name is slightly better. Kinda sounds like a noise Bobby McFerrin would make. What happened to Bobby McFerrin? He's probably in Florida, huh? Guns are good in the right hands—nobody's. What's on Larry King's mind these days? Anything facile and trite? When will RATT reunite? Where? I want the exact time and address because I don't want to be within fifty miles of that ground zero. Fewer carbs, more protein is yesterday's news. Have you ever asked someone you don't know how to refrigerate venison? Don't. It's a waste of time.

As to your question: don't. Eat venison raw, as soon as you have it, right on the spot. To get the gamey taste out of your basement freezer, use Handi Wipes and gasoline.

Cheers,

Bob

. . .

Dear Bob:

My next-door neighbor has several enormous stacks of old news-papers littering his front yard and a huge pile of discarded maga-zines spilling out of his trash can. How can I persuade him to actually recycle these old papers and not just stuff them in the trash?

Regards,

Lori

Berkeley, CA

Dear LORI:

Now that's an acronym-name I can get behind! Very clever of you to write to me about your "neighbor." Ha ha. What, did you think you would publicly humiliate me? Ain't gonna happen, dearie. For your little trick, here's what you get: I'm going to start throwing my diapers in the yard, too. After I poo in them, not before.

Bob

...

Dear Bob:

I recently moved to Chicago, a boring, useless heap of a city. I have three years of school left here. How do you suggest I pass my time with-out going utterly insane, and perhaps have fun every once in a while?

Best,

Isabelle

Chicago, IL

Dear IZZY:

There, I gave you an acronym-ish name. Try it on, see if it "works." Have you ever been to a Cubs game? Try the deep-dish. Do you like white people playing the blues? How about white people listening to the blues? If "yes," you're all set. If "no," you gotta go. I lived in Chicago and had some good times there. I also felt alienated by the "Da Bears" mentality. Sorry to bring up that *Saturday Night Live* sketch I helped write. Who invented the phrase "my bad"? That was "their bad" for sure.

Bob

. . .

Dear Bob:
I'm a Jew who doesn't agree with the politics in Israel. When I explain this to my Jewish friends, they say I'm a self-hating Jew and anti-Semitic. But isn't that as absurd as calling somebody unpatriotic for not blindly supporting the Bush administration?
A Jew Without a Country

Dear Jew-ish Person:
What do you think about a professional indoor baseball league? You hit the ball over a certain mark on the wall and get a home run. We could call it the I.B.L. and play all winter. Sound good? I thought of it first, right here. Also, put cheese on your apple pie; you'll thank me. Maybe. Then again, don't. I believe the Jews need a homeland, and it is a struggle to establish one in the modern world. It's always been a struggle to establish one. Someone always gets shafted. Do you consider yourself an American? Did anyone get screwed when this country was established? What's that? An entire nation of peoples was wiped out? That sounds pretty bad. Oh well, who won *American Idol*? I'll tell you who: everyone who watched.

Bob

John Oliver

Dear John:
The future is unknowable, the past is regrettable. How do you reconcile the present and get dinner on the table?
                                    Mike Rose
                                    Albuquerque, NM

Dear Mike:
First of all, you may be under the impression that you have blown my mind with that question. You would be wrong.

As a citizen of New Mexico, I'm not sure you should be concerning yourself too much with the future. Why? You people live in a desert. I would imagine that you are already in the process of preparing for your *Mad Max*–style existence, which will be taking place at some point in the next two to five years. When oil hits five dollars a barrel, make sure that you've got your spiky shoulder pads and face paint ready. It's Thunderdome time.

As for putting dinner on the table—let's not sugarcoat this. You're going to be living on roadkill. My advice would be "Always remove the squirrel's tail." That's a memory of cuteness you do not want to conjure up as you raise the stick toward your mouth.

All the best,
John

...

Dear John:
I love my mom, don't get me wrong. She birthed me and everything and I really appreciate that. But lately she's been getting on my nerves. How the hell do you break up with your mom?
Jan D.
Barrington, RI

Dear Jan D.:
First of all, thank you for your letter. In this age of e-mail, it is refreshing to receive correspondence written in fine ink on parchment, rolled up in a ribbon, and dropped into my lap by a finely dressed pigeon. That's not old-fashioned; that's just good manners.

Now, to your question, which is a good one. Opinion is split as to how long you are in debt to your mother for forcing you through her birth canal in an exercise so painful it makes you doubt both intelligent design and evolution. Some say five years. Others say three hundred. Personally, I say that we live in an age of rampant capitalism, and if your mother is not performing, you are well within your rights to terminate your contract of affection and seek another maternal figure in your life. That's just the system correcting itself. With luck, this will serve as a significant enough incentive to encourage your mother to up her game. Be warned, however; capitalism is a two-way canal. She is free to fire you if she feels that as a son you may be failing. And if this letter comes up at your performance review/tribunal, you are in serious trouble.

Good luck,
John

...

Dear John:
Is there really a difference between Modern Romance Glamour and Mid-Century Architecture?

Paul M.
Chesapeake, VA

Dear Paul M.:
None whatsoever. They both come under the banner "Trump chic."

John

...

Dear John:
The last time I visited New York, I bought a pair of knockoff Ugg boots from a street vendor. Now my sister tells me they're probably not made of sheepskin at all, and according to her they feel more like pug. This makes me sad, but I just love the way I look in my Uggs. What should I do?

Donna
Eau Claire, WI

Dear Donna:
Walk tall, and walk comfortably. There is absolutely nothing wrong with slipping your feet into "Ugg-inspired" shoewear, lined with purest, softest pug. You have to understand that

Ugg boots are originally from Australia, where sheep are everywhere. You bought those boots in New York, where we have very few sheep, but thousands upon thousands of pugs. We have a supply-and-demand situation there. I believe the boots you bought are even officially called "pUggs." Ugg boots are always made from animals native to the area; I believe in L.A. they are made from Chihuahuas and are called "chiwUggs."

And if anyone criticizes you for your footwear of choice, merely invite them to try them on. Before they know it, they'll be experiencing a full body shoegasm and booking a flight to New York.

> Yours,
> John

...

Dear John:
I've got about six pounds of grass cuttings in my garage and no clue what to do with it. Any ideas?

> *Dr. L. Harrison*
> *Seattle, WA*

Dear Dr. L. Harrison:
I will personally give you fifteen dollars if you cover yourself head to toe in glue, roll around in the grass cuttings, and go running down your street screaming, "Look at me; I'm a sticky wicket!" You may be jeopardizing your right to practice medicine, but I'm guessing that you're one of those "I'm-a-doctor-of-Shakespeare-not-a-real-doctor" doctors. So you don't really have much to lose.

I have two fives and five ones with your name on them. Your move.

> John

Patton Oswalt

Dear Patton:
How does one make a Spanish tortilla? I keep trying, and somehow end up with scrambled eggs and home fries. Help!
                                                    Rick
                                                    Allentown, PA

Dear Rick:
If you focus on your destination, then the journey will betray you. Many a traveler has set off for El Dorado and wound up at a discount hotel. Do not start with ground corn, water, and spices. Depart them, wordlessly, and make the tortilla seek you out. There will break a dawn when you will find yourself on a street in Venice. A radio will play a song you'd forgotten you'd remembered. Turn around twice. Embrace your fear. That's when the tortilla will hand you an umbrella.
                                                    Patton

...

Dear Patton:
I have a really nice ass, but I don't have a boyfriend. Why can't I get someone to love me?

Hope
Denver, CO

Dear Hope:
'Cause it's 2010, the year of the killer rack. 2009 was the year of the really nice ass. Wait till it cycles around again in 2015.

Patton

...

Dear Patton:
My neck is super sore after a night of dancing. How can I find out why this is the case?

Harry
Houston, TX

Dear Harry:
A night of dancing? In Houston? Be happy it's only your neck that's sore.

Patton

...

Dear Patton:
There's a nice, small, family-run grocery store on my block. Recently I've been reading about the upsides of feeding your dog real food, not the cardboard that passes for "dog food." Anyway, I fed him some carrots and beef from this grocery store and now my dog is dead. Do

you think I could sue the grocery store, and is it possible to sue for a new dog?

> *Warm regards,*
> *James David Lighton*
> *Florence, SC*

Dear Mr. Lighton:
"Carrots and beef"? I'm going to assume you served your dog sliced carrots and some sort of ground beef, possibly chuck. Quaint, tasty, and simple, yes? It's clear your dog died not from any food-borne illness but from mortification. Any pairing of a root vegetable with "upper-half" meats (chuck, rib, short loin, the three sirloins, and round) should also include a dark, bitter vegetable to counteract the intensity of the beef and the sweet/starchy quality of the root vegetable. When your dog realized he was forever shackled to such a culinary philistine, he surely willed his bodily functions to cease.

I shudder to think of your idea of a wine pairing. The poor mutt probably died with the sad tang of an overpriced Nebbiolo on his tongue.

> Patton

...

Dear Patton:
When I moved into my house, the former occupants notified me that the trees in the backyard were lemon trees. However, the fruits so far have been small, green, and hard, and give all indications of actually being limes. Is there a way to determine whether these are undernourished lemons or impostors?

> *Thanks,*
> *Margaux*
> *Santa Clarita, CA*

Dear Margaux:

Trying to taste the difference between a lemon and a lime? It's the age-old conundrum, and also a swell XTC lyric! Hey, why doesn't XTC tour anymore? Someone told me Andy Partridge was afflicted with crippling stage fright, but then someone else told me he's kind of an asshole and doesn't like his bandmates. Either way, it doesn't stop *Drums and Wires* from being one of my favorite albums. And all that nonsense about *Skylarking* being overproduced makes me want to throw a tin toy at a policeman! "Another Satellite" is a perfect, soaking-in-a-hot-tub-at-the-end-of-a-hard-day groove. And don't even get me started on "Summer's Cauldron"!

Patton

...

Dear Patton:

I have what I believe is an unnamed phobia and I'm looking for some insight. I can't bear to see my "bite mark" or rather "teeth profile" left behind when a piece of food is set back upon a plate. This usually occurs after the first bite of, for example, a piece of toast. Cream cheese only makes it worse. I then respond by quickly nipping the corner or edge off of the offensive shape with another, smaller bite. Thoughts?

Rob

Spokane, WA

Dear Rob:

Oh. My. God. After all these years of searching, hoping to avenge the death of my sister. The Neatly Nibbled Morsel Killer, falling into my trap. Stay right where you are, fiend!

Patton

...

Dear Patton:

Do you know of a full-body ergonomic sling I could drape myself in while typing? Something that could keep me suspended in a position of bliss and faux-zero G? Even now, as I type these words with one finger (it's a quick finger!), I feel shooting pains lancing up my wrists and through my shoulders, causing a cascade of aches to shudder across my back. My lower back is a repository of pain. Also, I think my left leg is shorter than my right.

> *Un-ergonomic Ursula*
> *Minneapolis, MN*

Dear U. U.:

Huh. Besides the Belly-Down Typ-o-matic BlissCradle from WombCrave Office Furniture, I'm drawing a blank. Sorry.

> Patton

. . .

Dear Patton:

I've been feeling blue lately but I wasn't sure if it had anything to do with the amount of rain we've had over the last few weeks. What are your thoughts on that?

> *Ms. Diller*
> *Cary, NC*

Dear Ms. Diller:

Rain can have a profound effect on someone inclined toward melancholy. I live in Los Angeles, and, as of this writing, we've just experienced three weeks of unending late-winter storms. The sky has been a limitless bowl of sludgy, hopeless gray. The ground, soaked and muddy, emits burbly, hissing spurts with every step, which sound like a scornful parent who sees no worth, hope, or value in their offspring. The morning light through my bedroom window promises nothing but a damp, unwelcoming day of thankless busywork and futile, doomed chores. My breakfast cereal tastes like being ostracized. My morning coffee fills my stomach with dread. What's the point of even answering this question?

The rain—it will not stop. Even if I say something that will help you—which I won't, because I'm such a useless piece of shit—you'll eventually die and I'll die and everyone we know will die and this book will turn to dust and the universe will run down and stop and dead dead dead dead dead.

Dead. Read *Chicken Soup for the Soul*, I guess. Dead. Dead dead.

Patton

Martha Plimpton

Dear Martha:

I really enjoy a nice peach, but I've been finding that they're too embarrassing to eat in public. Do you have any tips on how this most mighty of fruits can be munched upon and my dignity remain intact?
Thanks,
Sophie
Ogden, UT

Dear Sophie:
I'm glad you asked this. Women should never do anything in public that will upset the gentle facade of femininity that makes them attractive to potential husbands. I keep telling women this, and they don't listen, because they aren't very bright. Eating, talking, moving the muscles in your face in any way other than to produce a visage of contented adoration, pooping: these are everyday common mistakes women

make that keep them alone and ensure their solitude in old age. If you want to find a husband, eat a banana, seductively, using your tongue a lot, with no shirt on. Hope this helps!

Love,
Martha

...

Dear Martha:
My aunt and uncle are filthy rich. They buy Jet Skis and imported Italian wine and Ferraris and Cohibas. They're old and wrinkly and I'm young and hunky. But somehow, they've got all the material wealth and I've got squat. Any suggestions for sabotaging their lives and stealing their money?

Poor in Pottawatomie County, KS

Dear Poor in:
You're a horrible person, but I like you, so I'm going to give you some advice: First of all, you've got it backward. If you sabotage your rich relatives' lives before you steal their money, they won't have any money to steal, because you will have already sabotaged their lives, which will lead to money-lessness. Are you following me? You have to understand certain things if you're going to be a greedy bastard. Also, I need more information. You see, I have some diamond certificates tied up in a Nigerian bank account, and in order to withdraw them the bank requires a U.S. bank routing number and $50,000. For your help I will gladly reimburse you and your aunt, plus pay you 50 percent of my diamond wealth, which is roughly $8,397,432.27. What is your aunt's e-mail address?

Warmest regards,
Martha

...

Dear Martha:
My sister has alopecia, a disease that causes hair loss. The doctors
have told her it's incurable, so she's invested in a realistic-looking
wig. Unfortunately, her alopecia has also caused her eyebrows to
disappear. She usually just draws her own with an eyebrow pencil,
which is okay if she's able to take her time and really do it right.
But when she's in a hurry, she can end up looking surprised or
annoyed. How can I delicately tell her that her eyebrows scare me?
                                        Lisa Lhormer
                                        Raleigh, NC

Dear Lisa:
People who have no hair at all are the luckiest people in the
world. They're the human versions of Wooly Willy, that
novelty game with the cartoon guy's head that you put hair
on in different shapes with a magnet. What's more fun than
that?

Many impressive people are hairless, and proudly so.
There is even a tiny movement of alopecics who encourage
"Hairless Pride." Some people have eyebrows implanted into
the flesh on their foreheads. Tell your sister not to limit herself. There are plenty of places on Fourteenth Street in Manhattan where inexpensive fake eyebrows can be purchased.
She can even pick up a fun rabbi beard! The point is: mix it
up. New facial hair every day! Then, instead of scaring you,
she can make you laugh. Everybody wins!
                                        Martha

...

Dear Martha:

Even though I eat multiple times a day, I still get hungry. No matter how much I eat, I'm always hungry again. I've started to skip meals because, really, what's the difference? I'll just be hungry again in a few hours. Do you have any advice for me?

Emmanuel Stevens
Miami, FL

Dear Emmanuel:

OMG, have you seen *Lust, Caution*? The movie is kind of so-so, but Tony Leung is so good in it! I'm completely obsessed with him now. Let's not even discuss the sex scenes in that movie. Cannot even. He's a huge star in Hong Kong, of course, and he's been in a thousand movies and worked with every great Hong Kongese director ever in the history of Hong Kong. I swear to gawd, I think he's one of the greatest actors in the world, ever, and I have to marry him immediately!

Martha

Harold Ramis

Dear Harold:
I recently signed up for a Jewish dating site on the Internet. I wrote
in the "About Me" section that I enjoy reading The New Yorker.
My friend told me that makes me seem like a pompous ass whom no
one would ever want to date, much less come to love in the future. Is
she right? What should I say instead?

Most sincerely,
Estella
St. Louis, MO

Dear Estella:
Jewish guys love a little pompous ass; we're just afraid to ask
for it. Let it be known that you also give head, and no Jewish guy will care what you read.

Harold

...

Dear Harold:
Is there any part of the body that shouldn't, under any circumstances, be pierced?

                              Jewel C.
                              Greensboro, NC

Dear Jewel:
I'm a firm believer that no part of my body should be pierced, but if you insist on having it done, the one part I'd advise against piercing is the brain.

                              Harold

...

Dear Harold:
Last night while I was entertaining friends in another room, a stray cat scaled the side of my apartment, climbed in through my living room window, and did it with my seven-month-old cat. True story. My question is, am I going to be a bad father?

                              Stephen T.
                              Dayton, OH

Dear Steve:
You're not going to be the father; the stray cat is. Humans can't procreate with cats or indeed any other mammals.

                              Harold

...

Dear Harold:
Is pigweed poisonous? And, coincidentally, does it exist?
                                        Anonymous
                                        Cleveland, OH

Dear Anonymous:
I believe I smoked some pigweed at Woodstock. I don't think it was poisonous but I freaked out and woke up in the woods with about a pound and a half of truffles beside me and lots of mud on my nose. Janis Joplin was lying next to me with no pants on and a bottle of Jack Daniel's in her hand. David Crosby was lying on the other side of me wearing two pairs of pants. Janis immediately wanted to do more "pig" but I convinced her to just stick to booze, acid, pot, PCP, STP, DMT, MDA, mandrax, desoxyn, meth, Ritalin, coke, heroin, and ludes. That bitch could party! Anyway, when we got back to the tent, Hendrix wouldn't leave us alone. "Where you guys goin'? What's happening? Can I come? Got any pigweed?" So desperate, so sad. By the time we left Woodstock, I just felt totally burned out and haven't touched the "pig" since. Now, forty years later, it's all about pigweed at colleges and high schools, even in some progressive Montessori, Steiner, and Waldorf schools. But I tell the kids, "Stay off the pig." It killed Janis and Jimi and Ritchie Valens and the Big Bopper and Kurt Cobain and Sid Vicious and now they're dead and can't party anymore, let alone make records. Or CDs, I guess. Bummer.
                                        Harold

...

Dear Harold:
Is it wrong to use a fake ID to make a hot waitress think you're
younger than you actually are? I just like the way "age: 25" looks
on a license, and it makes me feel flirty. So sue me.

> J.D.
> *Chicago, IL*

Dear J.D.:
It's not wrong; it's just pathetic. If you look young enough to
pass for twenty-five, who gives a shit how old you actually are?
I'm currently buying movie tickets at the "senior citizen"
price and feeling good when they ask to see my ID, so fuck
you. But I know what you mean. I feel so much more flirty
when people think I'm only sixty-two. And surprise! I just
filed a lawsuit against you in the Cook County Circuit Court.

> Harold

...

Dear Harold:
What happens after you die?

> *Trevor Chartman, age 9*
> *Little Rock, AR*

Dear Trevor:
It all depends. If you're a Christian, it might be Heaven or
Hell. If you're Jewish, you get a brass plaque on a bench in
the synagogue if your kids aren't too cheap to make a nice
contribution. If you're a Hindu, you'll come back in a karmi-
cally appropriate incarnation. If you're a Buddhist, it doesn't
matter. And if you're an atheist, your body just rots in a hole
in the ground or gets toasted to ashes in a very hot oven. And
that's it.

The better question is, "What happens *before* you die?"
That's where we run into most of the problems.

Harold

...

Dear Harold:

*I am a recent college graduate (thanks!), and my dad says I should
go into plastics. What can you tell me about the advantages of this
industry in comparison to the advantages of youthful rebellion?*

Jonas Baker
Alpena, MI

Dear Jonas:

The advantages of youthful rebellion are overrated. Yes,
you could topple the capitalist system, oust the Pope, end
the use of drift nets in the tuna fishing industry, or install
Sharia law and a Taliban-style government, but so what?
What plastics has to offer is the possibility of replacing
organic life with a material that won't shrink, fade, or biode-
grade, available in all colors, shapes, and sizes, and resistant
to global warming, environmental degradation, and nuclear
winter.

Gotta love that.

Harold

...

Dear Harold:

*If Jews and Muslims were born of the same tribes of Jacob or Isaac
or Ronny or whoever killed Jesus, then why are they still fighting
today? Also, I can't get my potato latkes to come out tender on the*

*inside and crispy on the outside like my mother can. Is it something
I'm doing wrong with the flour?*

> *Ben Siegel*
> *Williamsville, NY*

Oy, Benny, Benny, Benny,
It's not the flour. The oil has to be very, very hot to quickly
caramelize the outside of the latke without overcooking the
inside. Try heating the oil to about 1,200 degrees (it should
be hot enough to melt an aluminum spatula), but be careful
when you drop the batter into the pan. You could be badly
burned. To be safe, let one of your gentile friends or a
schwarzer drop the batter in.

Now, as to why Jews and Muslims are still fighting when
we have a common ancestor in Abraham. Go figure. It can't
just be about the British giving Palestine to the Jews without consulting the indigenous people who occupied the land
continuously for the last nine hundred years after the dias-
pora. I think they just hate us because we're superior. Or is it
because we're inferior? I can't remember which. Either way,
why can't they just get over it already?

> Harold

. . .

Dear Harold:
*Do you ever hang out with other advice columnists? If so, what sorts
of things do you do together? What do you talk about?*

> *Joanna*
> *San Francisco, CA*

Dear Joanna:
Sometimes we do just hang out together, but the best is the
annual conference of advice-givers held once a year in Las

Vegas. What a blast! You might see Dan Savage of "Savage Love" talking to the guy from *Wine Spectator* about what Cabernet to drink with anal beads. Or Martha Stewart with the Playboy Advisor arguing about the best way to get cum stains out of a linen tablecloth. Or Suze Orman with Dr. Phil debating the wisdom of investing in anxiety futures. Or the gang from *Queer Eye* talking boxers vs. briefs with the *What Not to Wear* crew. After a few days you start to realize there's only so much advice you can take. What's that old saying? "Advice is like opinions. Everyone's an asshole."

Harold

Amy Sedaris

Dear Amy:
How should somebody go about bathing themselves? There are people on the street who smell horrible but you know they must shower. Is there some special inside thing we get that they don't?
Courtney Ivo
Chicago, IL

Dear Courtney:
Take a visit to your local animal shelter and pick up any random cat. Now take a deep whiff. Pretty sweet, right? It's called a tongue bath, and it's not just for felines anymore. In this fast-paced world, you'd be surprised at how many people are taking advantage of this superior and convenient form of bathing. But from the self-righteous tone of your

letter, I can only assume that you aren't one of them. For shame, Courtney. Why are you so afraid of your own tongue?

Amy

...

Dear Amy:

I want to be a fireman someday. I already have a fireman's uniform and it's super cool. Also, I've been practicing with a garden hose. But my parents don't think it's a good idea because of my asthma. Should I listen to them?

Kevin, age 8
Ann Arbor, MI

Dear Kevin:

Why don't you practice by setting a few rather large fires in your neighborhood? Find an abandoned warehouse and set it ablaze. Or better yet, burn down a coach house. Not only is it fun, but you can practice putting out the fires with the equipment you've started collecting. If you manage to save the buildings, then you're probably cut out to be a fireman. If you go into an asthmatic fit and have to be hospitalized, or get covered in third-degree burns and end up spending the rest of your life being fed by a tube, then maybe your parents were right after all. But you'll never know until you try.

Good luck and happy burning!

Amy

...

Dear Amy:

I've been single for about a year now, after a long-term relationship fizzled. All of a sudden, I'm starting to get those codependency urges again. Should I suppress these unwanted feelings without the use of pills or alcohol?

Sincerely,
Looking for an Out Without Slipping In

Dear Slippy:

What's wrong with pills and alcohol? Are you judging me? Whatever helps me through the hard times is a-okay with me. It kills the pain. I hate it when people start spewing out bullshit like, "You're going to have to deal with it sooner or later." Well, not really, because by the time "later" comes, my problem will be over because of the booze and pills. I'm not stupid. You codependent people are all the same!

Are you selling any pills?

Amy

...

Dear Amy:
They say that the fastest way to a man's heart is through his stomach. More specifically, what do you think is the best meal to serve my man to make sure he'll never, ever leave me?

Dani Kando-Kaiser
Sacramento, CA

Dear Dani:

First of all, I'm a bit of an amateur coroner. Let's just say I like to poke around. The fastest way to a man's heart is definitely through the chest cavity. Yeah, it's a bit of a bother sawing through all that bone, but trust me, it's a straight shot.

To answer your question about serving a dish that will keep your man happy, I suggest a Honey Baked west vagina ham, or turkey cordon blow him. Or how about chicken snatchatori?

Amy

. . .

Dear Amy:
I have a lot of white friends. Is it okay for white people to celebrate Kwanzaa with me?

Shaka Freeman
Oakland, CA

Dear Shaka:
A lot of white friends? Are you counting coworkers? Because technically, these people are not your friends. It's good politics to be friendly toward the people we work with. Remember that the next time you're gathered around the watercooler exchanging wacky weekend anecdotes. Why is this person being nice to me? What are they after? I'm sure excluding coworkers significantly whittles down your list of white "friends." But what about the white "friends" who are not coworkers? What's their deal? Well, they may maintain this relationship with you just so they can claim, "I've got a lot of black friends."

So you see, Shaka, you don't have a lot of white friends. I hope this solves your problem.

Amy

. . .

Dear Amy:
I hope you might be able to settle a bet. One of my friends insists that his Border collie (Henry) is smarter than my German shepherd

(Fuzz Head). In my opinion, Henry happens to be pretty dumb. He eats his own poo and pees uncontrollably when someone new enters the house. Is there some kind of reliable dog IQ test that we can administer to get to the bottom of this?

James Shoemaker
San Francisco, CA

Dear James:

First of all, if we judged intelligence solely on how much bodily waste one ingested, then I must be an idiot. It's called urine therapy. I drink all the urine I can get my hands on. Holy men in India have been doing it for thousands of years. Urine enhances beauty and cleanses the bowels. Mostly I drink the midstream of my morning pee. Occasionally I'll drink it steaming hot but usually I mix it with juice or enjoy it over fruit parfait. Although there is zero scientific evidence that drinking urine is beneficial to one's health, I choose to believe the opposite based on an uninformed whim. So now how stupid am I?

Getting back to your dog situation. Intelligence can be measured by problem-solving abilities; e.g., taking a regular swig of home brew to cure a malady. Create a problem for the dogs and see which one can solve it. Start a shed on fire, and then get inside and see which dog drags you to freedom. There is always the possibility that neither dog will come to your aid, but at least the world will be free of one more narrow-minded skeptic misjudging my prodigious intake of the precious salty nectar distilling between my loins.

Amy

...

Dear Amy:

I just lost $3,000 at an illegal cockfighting ring in Chiapas, Mexico. I want my money back, so naturally I'm going back in March. Are there any telltale signs of superior, aggressive, and more violent cocks?

> *Allan H.*
> *Amarillo, TX*

Dear Allan:

Ah, the sawdust, the flying feathers, the spraying blood. I imagine those are the precious memories I'd cherish about cockfighting, if I had indeed spent the bulk of the eighties cheering on my feisty squad of slashing gamecocks in the sweaty, dank basement of a Filipino named Sabong. But I am a lady, and I was probably doing something else.

Look, Allan, I don't know anything about the illegal and brutal sport of cockfighting, but I can tell you this: if you want to be a pit master when you return to Mexico, first gain some experience by attending the World Slasher Cup, an eight-cock derby held in a garage in Queens that any cocker worth his salt will be attending. Bet on the brood cocks because they are real glashers, often outfitted with Malaysian razor-sharp spurs or the Pakpak Langaw blade. They're sure to make an under hack out of any Manok. I'll see you there! Or rather, I won't.

> Amy

Sarah Silverman

Dear Sarah:
I came out to my family as a gay man nearly nine years ago. While they've become more accepting of me, they still hold out hope that I'll meet "the right woman." I've never seen a woman naked, let alone dated one. How can I avoid the "don't knock it if you haven't tried it" argument and convince my family that I'm just not into girls?
Nathan Yergler
Fort Wayne, IN

Dear Nathan:
First of all, did they not knock homosexuality before they tried it? Exactly. They're asking you to be open-minded so they don't have to. You can always lie and say, "Mom, I had sex with a woman and it was awful! Vaginas are gross! I'm glad I tried it but I'm gonna stick with penis. What's for dinner?" Another idea is to adopt a baby. Once there's a baby

in the picture, they don't care who you're fucking. They just want to squeeze that little tushy!

Sarah

...

Dear Sarah:
I think saffron looks so attractive in its tiny plastic cage at the supermarket, but I really have no idea what one might do with it. Any ideas?

Sammy Chafos
New York, NY

Dear Sammy:
I had some saffron rice this very morning, and it looked so yellow and so yummy, but it tasted like a doodie flower. I kept eating it because after each bite, my eyes would glance back at the plate and I'd get seduced all over again. My advice is to enjoy it in the market. Awe in its pure yellow intensity the way you may take in a painting or a gossip rag at the checkout stand. Then walk away.

Sarah

...

Dear Sarah:
My mom always gives me a hard time for having the day off from school on Labor Day. She tells me, "I'm the one who went into labor to have you, and I don't have the day off!" What would be a good comeback that I could say to her next year?

Jimmy Whealdon
Irvine, CA

Dear Jimmy:
Don't say anything. Just kick her in the vagina. Then, as she keels over, point to her vagina and start to laugh, but then freeze, like you're in the end credits of *Bob Newhart* or *CHiPs* or *Barney Miller*. If she doesn't "get it," then she's not worth your time anyway.

Sarah

...

Dear Sarah:
I'm a happily married man, but lately one of my golfing buddies, Jerome (not his real name), has been acting a bit peculiar around me: holding the door open for me, picking up the bar tab, and look-ing at me in, well, a way that makes me feel kind of weird. Jerome isn't married and hasn't had a girlfriend since I can remember. I can tell sometimes that Jerome has something he wants to tell me. My question is, when Jerome and I have secret sex at the hourly motel, who should pay for the room?

Jim (not my real name)
Sonoma, CA

Dear Jim:
You are so lucky that I went to gay charm school. The top pays for the motel.

Sarah

...

Dear Sarah:
I've recently moved to New York City from California. Everything is great but I'm having trouble adjusting to my new habitat. I feel

as if I'm an animal on display but without a handful of feces to protect myself. What should I do?

Jordan Farray
New York, NY

Dear Jordan:
This is a tough one. I love New York, but you get more space in L.A., so it can be a pleasant experience just to hang in and be home. In New York, unless you're rich, you live in a very small space, so your instinct is to get out until you have to come home to sleep. Try to nest. Make your apartment as homey and comfortable as possible—a little haven. Or just shit in your hand.

Sarah

. . .

Dear Sarah:
I'm a chronically depressed shut-in who doesn't bathe much. My lifestyle has caused a testicular fragrance of vast proportions. What should I do?

Chris Heffernan
Long Island, NY

Dear Chris:
You may think you're a shut-in and that therefore you don't wash your balls. But I'm here to tell you that you are a shut-in *because* you don't wash your balls. If you wake up and jump in the shower—or better yet, laze in a tub—by the time you get out and towel off, you are much more apt to feel like going out into the world. This is not a chicken-and-egg scenario. Trust me: balls first, and your life will follow.

Sarah

Paul F. Tompkins

Dear Paul:
When there's food in my office, I'll eat it all, regardless of how many cashews I ate on the way to work. How do I stop myself from compulsively overeating?

Doug Prentiss
Santa Fe, NM

Dear Doug:
Wait, wait, wait. How much food is in this office? How much could there be? Do you people work more than eight hours? Do you work on an oil rig? You're very mysterious about the food and how it gets into the office. Are you eating your coworkers' stuff? Not cool. Confess that you've been eating their Lean Pockets and the overeating will stop when they knock your teeth out. Do you work alone and suddenly food is just . . . there? Perhaps you are a sleepy cobbler and the

industrious elves, in addition to doing your job, are leaving behind deli trays and pudding packs. I don't know the situation. If you won't be straight with me, the best I can do is advise you to give up on that cashew-as-appetite-suppressant plan. I think those nuts are just whetting your appetite for all the food that is contained in a building.

Paul

...

Dear Paul:

I've been infected with poison oak or ivy. Research and doctors have told me that there is no cure and I will suffer from constant itching, oozing, and blisters for the next two to three weeks. I don't believe the doctors. I think they are hiding something just so those of us who are highly allergic to this evil plant can suffer. Do you know of home remedy that will make the pain go away?

Jennifer
Austin, TX

Dear Jennifer:

I fear for your safety now that you have revealed this conspiracy. Poison oak is the least of your problems. You'd better get out of the country and I mean now. Also, I'm mocking you. Stop being ridiculous! That's what the doctor cabal picked as the official affliction they're gonna fold their arms over and do nothing about? Do you know how many kinds of insane cancers there are out there that they've probably just given up on? Come on. Tough it out. Watch where you're walking next time. Also, "Do you know of home remedy"? Did you think talking like a villager in an old *Wolfman* movie would make me cough up some secret Gypsy cure?

Paul

...

Dear Paul:

My roommates and I have trouble making friends. We recently moved to a new city and every time we go out and meet new people, we never hear from them again. We are getting tired of hanging out with each other. How do we get these people to be friends with us without coming across like stalkers or cult {sic}?

> Peter Green
> San Francisco, CA

Dear Peter:

Maybe these people are picking up on the obvious hatred you and your roommates have for each other. It seems like you all would be better off away from each other, finding your own individual pals instead of surrounding innocent people and forcing your gang-friendship down their throats. Divide and conquer. Give San Francisco a break.

Oh, and "coming across like stalkers or cult"—who are your roommates? Jennifer from Austin? Borat? Tonto?

> Paul

...

Dear Paul:

Smoking marijuana makes me afraid of everything. I still love to joke about it, though, and talk about it all the time, and end up smoking it at every opportunity. How do I kick the habit?

> Marsha Knesbitt
> Colorado Springs, CO

Dear Marsha:

If I had to listen to you make a bunch of tired, unfunny pot jokes and endure endless hours of your yammering about pot and how great it is and how it needs to be legalized and how you can make clothes out of hemp and glaucoma blah blah blah, and then found out you didn't even smoke pot anymore, I would murder you and then kill myself. Don't kick the habit. For both our sakes.

Paul

...

Dear Paul:
I just moved into a new apartment and my room is right off of the living room. My roommates watch a lot of TV, always after mid-night and always very, very loudly. I hate my new roommates. Should I just move out or sit down with them and try to defuse the situation?

Smiles,
Greg Klondike
Dublin, CA

Dear Greg:
Ha! Are you talking about calling a "house meeting"? That is rich! Those never work! Never! You will only be left with the cold comfort afforded you by having taken the high road, while your roommates label you an uptight, patronizing old grandma. And they will start eating your organic peanut butter out of the communal fridge like a pack of Doug Prentisses.

If you can drive the thirty-six miles from Dublin to San Francisco, there is an awesome roommate situation waiting for you! Greg, you are just what those Moonies need to shake things up! Pack up your earplugs and persecution complex and hit the road!

Paul

Sarah Vowell

Dear Sarah:

Over the last few months, I've developed a crush on a librarian. He's not exactly a hottie, but there's something about him that I find irresistible. Maybe it's the argyle sweater or the pear-shaped body. It just drives me wild. But I don't have the guts to ask him out. Do you have any suggestions?

Kelly Lawson
Salt Lake City, UT

Dear Kelly:

Why not enlist his help on a research project explaining the etymology and implications of the phrase "Adlai Stevenson moment"? This might allow you (a) the hair-sniffingly close physical proximity involved with the presentation of research materials—and here I suggest, assuming his library has yet to transfer its analog collections to digital, that you "accidentally" drop a roll of microfilm, unspooling it across the room so the two of you, on all fours, can rewind it together—and (b) a casual way to assess his position on verbal bravery. Like, if he seems turned on by Stevenson's rhetorical gumption toward Soviet ambassador Zorin in 1962, he might be similarly impressed if you ask him out in 2009. If he hesitates to answer, just bark, as Stevenson did so famously and so adorably, "Don't wait for the translation—yes or no?" He will be very charmed by this, especially if you follow up with black-and-white aerial photographs of possible first-date locations. If you have limited helicopter access, you may simply type in the library's ZIP code and order one of the U.S. Geological Survey's photos taken from 20,000 feet (www.usgs.gov).

Sarah

...

Dear Sarah:
I have an abundance of dryer lint in all different shades of grays and whites. I usually fashion baby wigs with the stuff. Can you suggest other creative uses for my fuzzy matter?

Gary Brewer
Mesa, AZ

Dear Gary:
I cannot. However, I would caution you to remember it's not the destination but the journey where dryer lint, like so many things in life, is concerned. According to the Consumer Product Safety Commission, there are more than fifteen thousand dryer fires every year in the United States, causing tens of millions of dollars in damages. So your seemingly stupid hobby turns out to be quite civic-minded and safety-firsty. Way to go, you!

Sarah

. . .

Dear Sarah:
I've found lately that the hints I read from Heloise every Sunday in
the newspaper are becoming less funny and more useful. Am I getting
old, or just more practical?

Jamie Spears
Aspen, CO

Dear Jamie:
I wouldn't know. My hometown newspaper, a little old rag
called the *New York Times*, does not stoop to publishing
comic strips or ladylike advice columns, unless you count
the op-ed pages under the current reign of editorial page editor Ms. Gail Collins. At press time, Ms. Collins's page coun-
sels our president to dissuade his visiting Nigerian colleague
Olusegun Obasanjo from amending the Nigerian constitution to allow for a third presidential term, a "foolhardy" tactic the *Times* fears will spark a civil war. Advice which, to
answer your question, is both practical and hilarious, except
for the glaring omission of how club soda might also help.

Sarah

. . .

Dear Sarah:
As a sales representative for a large pharmaceutical concern, I spend a
considerable portion of my day behind the wheel and have taken to
preparing hot meals on the engine block of my company-issued
automobile. The meats and shellfish come out just fine, but I'm having
trouble with the grilled asparagus. I'm not sure if I'm wrapping the
foil too tightly, or if my choice of olive oil is to blame. Please help.

Thomas Mullen
Washington, DC

Dear Thomas:

Gee, that's terrific that you can take time out of your busy schedule of turning America's elderly into Canadian drug smugglers while further guzzling the gas that ensures our dependence on foreign oil and simultaneously contributes to the global warming that will eventually drown the entire tristate area so as to Alice Waters up your otherwise Willy Loman existence. According to Ms. Waters's *Chez Panisse Vegetables*, she parboils asparagus spears in boiling salt water for one minute before throwing them onto a grill.

Sarah

. . .

Dear Sarah:

I am an Orthodox Christian and have always dated Orthodox guys until now. I met a wonderful man at Trader Joe's and am now head over heels in love. My family won't accept our relationship, however, and now I don't know what to do. Should I break up with him in order to please my family?

Kate Mobley
Portland, OR

Dear Kate:

A Trader Joe's just opened here in Manhattan! What are their snacks you recommend? I remember enjoying some of their cheddar soy crisps in the Bay Area a couple of book tours ago, thanks to a thoughtful media escort who uses the phrase "socially conscious" more than one hears back east, but lately I have more of a thing for sweet potatoes.

Sarah

. . .

Dear Sarah:

I recently celebrated a milestone birthday (the big four-oh!) and I'm suddenly plagued with self-doubt. I guess you could say that I'm part of the so-called intellectual elite. I read several books a day, I'm fluent in five languages, and I regularly attend the opera. But since my birthday, I've become acutely aware of my shortcomings. I don't know how to change the oil in my car, for instance. And I don't enjoy professional sports. Is this something I should be concerned about?

Jason Sanders
New York, NY

Dear Jason:

Is one of the languages you speak pussy? I ask you: What requires more masculine stamina, lollygagging on a couch in one's pajamas during the NBA play-offs while receiving constant noisy sustenance from the good people of Frito-Lay, or sitting in a stiff seat wearing a stiff tuxedo suffering through two straight nights of Wagner's eleventy-hour Ring Cycle and getting the evil eye from stout divas in horned helmets if you so much as unwrap a cough drop? And if you really want to learn how to change the oil in your (lemme guess) Saab, I'm thinking a guy who's managed to effortlessly conjugate five kinds of subjunctive verbs can speed-read *Auto Repair for Dummies*, for crying out loud. Plus, according to Camus's *The Myth of Sisyphus* (*Le Mythe de Sisyphe* to you), "There is but one truly serious philosophical problem, and that is suicide." Hope that cheers you up—if you'll pardon my split infinitive.

Sarah

David Wain

Dear David:
Lately my wife has been withdrawn and pretty bummed out. When I ask her what's wrong, she says, "For no particular reason." Is she mad at me?

Eric Fetterman
New York, NY

Dear Eric:
You have obviously not yet learned the fine art of "reading" women. A woman is a creature that can be studied. It took me years, both in the United States and in Sun City, but now I know—I mean *really know*—women. The benefits of this knowledge are endless: hours of achingly lurid sex; meals cooked at the snap of a finger any time of day or night (and I'm not just talking about the standard meat loaf. Try these sample dishes on for size: caramelized beef au jus in a blazed

reduction of rice and cream; tuna à la king; Moroccan noodle surprise; chocolate cake—and that's only a sampling). In your case, the read could not be easier: Your wife's refrain of "For no particular reason" is a thinly veiled signal that she wants you to take her to a rodeo. I promise you, after one afternoon of ridin' and ropin' (and barrel racing), your wife will be chipper, horny, and ready to pork.

David

...

Dear David:

I've got a group of friends I really love. Unfortunately, some of them can end up playing mind games with each other and with me. How should I handle their aggressive or patronizing behavior?

Ian

San Francisco, CA

Dear Ian:

I assume by "mind games" you mean brain teasers. My advice is to simply break it down into pieces and make a chart. For example, if the butler is in the room next to Duane, then the butler cannot be Duane, so you just put an "X" on that part of the grid. If you keep eliminating all the possibilities, I'm confident you'll find that Mrs. Leeverlily was the only one in the study at the time of the murder and so she had the opportunity to shoot General Thornbush with the silver revolver and hide his body in the convertible couch.

If your friends are still patronizing after trying the above, they're not good friends and you should try to get some new ones. I suggest joining a club where you'll meet people with similar interests. In your case, check out the fag club.

Good luck!

David

...

Dear David:
My cat likes to eat raw cookie dough, so I often leave a few table-
spoons of it in her dish after I'm finished baking. Is this inhumane?
                                        Julia Mordaunt
                                        Burlington, VT

Dear Julia:
Oh, Julia. Where to start? First of all, just because she eats
cookie dough doesn't mean she likes it. She might eat it
because it's all she gets. Why don't you ever give her regular
cat food? Cookie dough is filled with sugar and carbs. At
least make it with Splenda and low-fat chocolate chips. Also,
why don't you call Richard back? He's so fond of you, and so
what if he was a little boring on the first date? He was probably nervous. He's a nice guy and he's got a good job, and it's
not like you've got men lined up around the block, no
offense. Would it kill you to just meet him again for a cup of
coffee and see if you might like him a little more? I hear he's
been rock climbing. Maybe you guys could go together. I
hate to see you always showing up alone at weddings. Give
him a call. I told him you would. Okay, that's it. I've said my
piece. I'll shut up now and you do what you want with your
life.

                                        Much love,
                                        David

...

Dear David:
I have a chronic problem. I'm always dropping things, or losing
things. At the bar or in my home, it doesn't matter. If there is a

liquid, I usually spill it. I was wondering, what is the best way to handle this?

Cory
Los Angeles, CA

Dear Cory:
Luckily, yours is a problem that has a simple solution. Stop being a putz! Let's role-play: You're in a nice restaurant and the waiter brings you a martini. You do not put the full martini glass in the breast pocket of your blazer! This is not as suave as you think it is. Plus, there's a very good chance the martini will spill. Better bet: keep the martini on the table and carefully sip it. Same goes for bug juice and Coke. Another tip: don't butter your honeydews. They're harder to keep a hold of, especially if you only have one hand. (Are you an amputee? Your letter didn't specify.) Keep on keeping on, Cory. I'm rooting for you, and so are all of my staff.

David

...

Dear David:
Is it ethical to dispose of one pet (dead) by feeding it to another?
Yulia Strizheus
Cicero, IL

Dear Yulia:
Yulia? That's your name? I'm not even going there, girl-friend. Anyway, regarding your question: in our family we had three ways of disposing of pets—flushing (for iguanas), burying (for dogs), and a bullet to the brain (for cats). Feeding one pet to another is barbaric, medieval, and sick. But with a name like Yulia, my guess is you're some kind

of dirty, scab-covered foreigner. So go ahead, knock yourself out.

> With great respect,
> David

...

Dear David:
Sometimes I like to surprise my wife and come home in the middle of
the day for lunch and a massage. But lately, when I arrive, I find
her playing around in the yard with Bosco, one of the neighborhood
dogs. He's a red-and-brown collie and he's friendly with everyone,
but there's something about the way he licks her knee that doesn't sit
right with me. What should I do?

> *Chris Heffernan*
> *Queens, NY*

Dear Chris:
As awkward as it sometimes can be, the only solution is to
sit down and have a heart-to-heart talk with Bosco. If he's
unresponsive (as collies can tend to be—I tell you from experience), then you'll have to be proactive and structure the
conversation. Give Bosco ample opportunity to tell you if
he's attracted to your wife, and if so, which parts of her
specifically. Be prepared: in situations like this, Bosco might
not offer much more than a "ruff-ruff" or "bow-wow." Don't
be discouraged by this. It could be the only way Bosco
knows how to communicate. Another tactic is to talk to your
wife about the situation. If she only offers you a "bow-wow,"
then my guess is your wife is something of a hound and
should be dropped faster than a hot potato.

> Much love,
> David

. . .

Dear David:
I only shave every three days. Do you think this is enough, or should
I do it more frequently?

> Jason McKinney
> Denver, CO

Dear Jason:
There was an old middle school rhyme I used to sing that's a
good rule of thumb:

> *Shave your beard every four days*
> *Balls every two*
> *Your butt is like another face*
> *And from it comes a doo.*

Follow these words and you, too, can enjoy the true relationship that I have with God.

> Keep in touch,
> David

. . .

Dear David:
I get really angry whenever I watch TV. Not just at the news, but
at sitcoms and dramas and pretty much everything that's on. I start
screaming and throwing things at the screen and my blood pressure
goes through the roof. Is this my problem or does TV owe me an
apology?

> Madsen
> Madison, WI

Dear Madsen:

There is an easy fix for this problem. First I'd suggest putting a tarp over the broken part of the roof, which will keep out rain and burglars (at least those without scissors). Next, mix a solution of plaster, cement, water, caulking grease, and stucco. Carefully spread this mixture across the roof-hole. To prevent your blood pressure from penetrating the roof again, I'd suggest steel reinforcements (3 x 5), which you can ask for at your local reinforcements depot.

Sincerely,

David

P.S. If you want to get less angry when watching TV in the first place, try watching higher-numbered channels. I'm particularly partial to 359, 435, and 436.

P.P.S. Your TV does not "owe" you an apology or "owe" you anything. He must *choose* to apologize on his own, or what's it worth? Please tell him I'd be willing to do a phone session with him.

...

Dear David:

How long should you fight to save your marriage before you admit that you're really in love with alimony?

Madison K.

Austin, TX

Dear Madison:

Five weeks.

Best,

David

...

Dear David:
I'm willing to cook at home as long as what I cook doesn't resemble
a dead animal. But I hate doing dishes, and I especially hate the
smell that wafts up from a stack of dirty dishes overflowing from the
sink onto the counter. What do you recommend?

Christy
Danbury, CT

Dear Christy:
No one enjoys doing dishes. It's one of those universally hated tasks that we all have to deal with, especially folks like you and I who have an ongoing (if nonexclusive) love affair with the art of haute cuisine. It's basically a four-step process:

1. Cook (preferably something Thai or SoCal-LoCarb).
2. Eat (slowly—put your BlackBerry away!).
3. Relax, digest, enjoy a good sex pamphlet or take a crack at solving the Rubik's Snake.
4. Have the cleaning woman do the dishes.

Good luck,
David

ADDENDUM: Since this article was first published, I've received numerous inquiries from aspiring stay-at-home cooks who claim not to employ a cleaning woman, and/or whose cleaning woman doesn't work after dinner. First of all, are you joking? If you are not, then I'd suggest having your cleaning man do the dishes. If you have neither, then I think you have much bigger problems than a sinkful of dishes (e.g., dirty sheets).

Rainn Wilson

Dear Rainn:
I woke up this morning to find a mushroom growing out of my carpet. Should I call the landlord or just eat it?
Christine Ramos
Buffalo, NY

Dear Christine:
A mushroom is a fungus. When we visit zoos or botanical gardens and mushrooms are featured, the title of the exhibition always is "There's a Fungus Among Us!" Write the landlord a letter with that phrase title and he'll knowingly nod and take care of the situation.

Sidebar: contrary to popular mythology, *all* mushrooms are edible and actually quite nutritious, so feel free to pop that fuzzy sucker in your pie hole!
Rainn

...

Dear Rainn:
I have a crush on a girl I had a dream about last night. I don't think she even exists. How can I get in touch with her? She's the one for me!

> C. Williamson
> New York, NY

Dear C.:
Funny you should ask. I have created an all-purpose Web portal for interactions such as yours. It's called Dreamconnect.com. Simply describe your literal "dream" girl, and an e-mail blast will be sent out to our database of over eighty thousand girls who have enrolled on our site because they feel that they have been or will be "dreamed of." Our powerful search engine will match you to a selection of these "dream girls," and for $490 you will be able to contact what is sure to be the love of your life!

Note: most of our "dream girls" don't speak English, only Bulgarian, so good luck with that!

Also: I love the name Williamson. It's so simple. Son of William. Somewhere back in the old country there was a man named William and that man was your father.

> Rainn

...

Dear Rainn:
Is it okay to fart in yoga class?

> Karen Thurn
> San Jose, CA

Dear Karen:

According to Dave Finster of *Science on the Stairs*, when you fart, small molecules of fecal matter, methane, and intestinal tissue are disbursed into the air. When you fart in yoga class, what better way for people to get to know you than to breathe in your fecal molecules and embed them into their lungs? You will literally merge with your class and bring your souls together! Best to announce it first, though, so your classmates can begin their Pranayama™ techniques and link their mind, body, and spirit with your atmospheric fecal bounty.

Rainn

. . .

Dear Rainn:

I just got dumped by my shitty boyfriend who works with me. How do I get him fired and steal all of his friends and leave him in a watery grave while still maintaining a devil-may-care attitude? Also, please advise on revenge tactics.

Amanda
Long Beach, CA

Dear Amanda:

Press a knife into the center of his eye. It will go into his brain. See how far it can go. Make a tuxedo from his blood. Dance like you've never danced before. Take a tour of a museum that you've never been to before, like the Gene Autry Museum or the Museum of Fog. Watch *Inspector Gadget 2: Gadget Meets His Match*, starring French Stewart. Make something besides pesto from pine nuts and then . . .

I'm sorry, what was the question?

Rainn

...

Dear Rainn:
Is the Iraq War still going on? I keep forgetting.
                              Miriam Brooks
                              Fort Wayne, IN

Dear Miriam:
The war is indeed over and peace has been restored to the land. As a matter of fact, I've established the first Iraq scenic peace tours for concerned liberals. Just sign in at FertileCrescentTours.com and check out our guided walking tours of Fallujah and Mosul. We have amphibious duck boat tours of Ramadi that take you up and down the Tigris-Euphrates. (History's "Fertile Crescent" from history class!) Camp out under the stars in the glorious Anbar Province and take in the fresh sea air at the port of Basra. Tours start at nine thousand euros; sign up today!
                              Rainn

...

Dear Rainn:
What is the best way to get rid of a ghoul that lives in your home?
I think I've got one and it's totally fucking rude.
                              Cecile
                              Fort Worth, TX

Dear Cecile:
Ghoul catching instructions:
    1. One large wooden box covered in religious symbology.
    2. Place box on bed in bedroom. (Preferably child's bed.)
    3. One stick (10 inches).
    4. Prop up one end of said box with stick.

5. One string (10 feet).

6. Tie string to that stick.

7. Human baby blood (1 pint).

8. Pan or tub.

9. Place baby blood in said pan or tub.

10. Place pan or tub under box.

11. Hide in the closet and keep the other end of the string taut in your hand.

12. Peer through keyhole. When the ghoul starts to lap up the human baby blood, simply tug on the string, causing the stick to fall and the ghoul to be captured in the box!

13. Set fire to box and ghoul.

You're welcome.

Rainn

Lizz Winstead

Dear Lizz:
What happens when you throw a green rock into the Red Sea?
                              Esther
                              Decatur, IN

Dear Esther:
Like all rock throwing in the region, it will be greeted with
Israeli rocket fire and sanctions.
                              Lizz

...

Dear Lizz:
I hate my neighbors. How can I passive-aggressively let them know
how I feel?

                              Annoyed in Akron

Dear Annoyed:

Here's a great passive-aggressive technique I have always had luck with. Invite them to dinner, and while you are reminding them that you had asked for a Merlot but the Pinot Noir they brought will probably be okay, let the husband know you would have to drink three bottles of it before you could even think of having sex with his wife.

If that doesn't work, burn down their garage.

Lizz

. . .

Dear Lizz:

Do you know the origin of the phrase "head over heels"? My personal experience has taught me that most of our heads are usually over our heels, unless we are grotesquely deformed. So to say I am "head-over-heels in love" is basically like saying I am "hands-at-the-end-of-arms in love." Riiiiiiight?

Hannah Pantone
Salem, OR

. . .

Dear Hannah:

The origin of the phrase actually came from the era in our evolutionary process when Jesus rode dinosaurs, and the shinbone and foot grew out of the upper base of the skull. This is Science 101. So, Hannah, you are not "riiiiiiiight."

Lizz

. . .

Dear Lizz:

Sometimes, late at night, I'll sneak to the computer while my girl-friend is asleep and browse the army recruitment website. Should I set aside my beliefs against harming others, put my career plans on hold for three years, and risk the mind-fuck that comes with killing another human being? Somebody has to do it, right?

Morally Foggy in Northern California

Dear Foggy:

So many people don't explore their passion for bloodlust and sit back while others go for their dream of nurturing their inner killing machine. Harming others is fun. If they are stupid enough to let themselves be harmed, whose fault is it really?

So I say, "Go for it!" You've only got one chance on this earth. But when you go sign up, if you are gay in any way, *do not mention it*! K?

Lizz

...

Dear Lizz:

I'm interested in finding a new job in this shitty economy. Can you advise me which field to look for work in? I am good at nothing.

Kevin Albert
Oshkosh, WI

Dear Kevin:

I would recommend looking into opportunities in cable news or at the meatball bar at IKEA.

Lizz

...

Dear Lizz:
Whatever happened to skorts and slap bracelets? They were so cool.
                            Missing the good ol' days
                            Chicago, IL

Dear Missing:
Like all fashion trends that combine two cute garments into one hideous one, the skort was pushed into fashion oblivion by its newer cousin the "shant," the short/pant. And the shant is already in fashion's rearview mirror as trendsetters everywhere are sporting the "skump," the skirt/pump, and the "trong," the trouser/thong.

   As for the slap bracelet, I think you can read about where it ended up in paragraphs twelve and thirteen of the torture memos.

                            Lizz

                            . . .

Dear Lizz:
Which perfume is more likely to get me laid? Floral or food flavored?

                            Marianne Kuban
                            Fayetteville, AR

Dear Marianne:
Try to find a scent that combines both, like a Cool Ranch Patchouli.

                            Lizz

The Horrible People

Aziz Ansari can be seen in the NBC series *Parks and Recreation*, as well as movies such as *Funny People*; *I Love You, Man*; and *Observe and Report*. He's also one-third of MTV's hit sketch comedy series *Human Giant*.

Judd Apatow wrote and directed the films *Knocked Up* and *Funny People* and was the cowriter and director of *The 40-Year-Old Virgin*. He was also the executive producer of the television series *Freaks and Geeks*.

Fred Armisen is, among other things, a repertory cast member on *Saturday Night Live*. This may not still be true when you're reading this. Welcome to the future!

Maria Bamford stars in her own Web sitcom on SuperDeluxe .com and in Comedy Central's *Comedians of Comedy*. Her other appearances include *Late Night with Conan O'Brien*, *The Tonight Show with Jay Leno*, and *Comedy Central Presents . . . Maria Bamford*.

Todd Barry is a stand-up comedian who occasionally acts. He played Mickey Rourke's mean boss in *The Wrestler* and the annoying bongo player on *Flight of the Conchords*. He's done stand-up on *The Late Show with David Letterman* and *Late Night with Conan O'Brien*, and in two Comedy Central specials.

Samantha Bee is the Most Senior Correspondent at *The Daily Show with Jon Stewart*. She enjoys unicorn-themed collectibles and watching kittens play with balls of yarn.

Michael Ian Black and Michael Showalter are former and current members of the comedy troupes The State and Stella, performers in the cult movie *Wet Hot American Summer* (which Showalter also cowrote), and begrudging costars of the Comedy Central series *Michael & Michael Have Issues*.

Andy Borowitz is a writer and comedian whose work appears in *The New Yorker, The New York Times*, and at his award-winning humor site, BorowitzReport.com.

Michael Cera was a cast member of the short-lived TV show *Arrested Development* and has appeared in the movies *Superbad, Juno, Nick and Norah's Infinite Playlist, Year One, Paper Heart*, and *Scott Pilgrim vs. the World*. He played Nick Twisp in the adaptation of *Youth in Revolt*.

Vernon Chatman and **John Lee** cocreated a show on MTV2 called *Wonder Showzen*, which featured puppets saying and doing horrible things.

Rob Corddry was a correspondent on *The Daily Show with Jon Stewart* for five years. He's appeared in movies such as *Old School, What Happens in Vegas, Harold & Kumar Escape from Guantanamo Bay*, and many others. He also stars in the WB Web series *Childrens' Hospital*.

David Cross was a runner-up at Seattle's Boeing Airplane Plant Hot Sauce Challenge for Charity 2002.

Larry Doyle, a former writer for *The Simpsons*, works in showbiz and writes funny things for *The New Yorker*. He lives outside Baltimore with his wife, Becky, their three children, and one dog, until it dies, and then no more dogs, according to the wife. His novel, *I Love You, Beth Cooper*, was made into a movie.

Paul Feig is the creator of the former NBC series *Freaks and Geeks*, as well as the director of the movies *I Am David* and *Unaccompanied Minors* and many episodes of the TV shows *Arrested Development* and *The Office*. He is also the author of the books *Kick Me, Superstud*, and *Ignatius MacFarland: Frequenaut!*

Jim Gaffigan is a stand-up comedian, actor, and writer. He can currently be seen on the third season of TBS's flagship comedy *My Boys* and in *17 Again* with Zac Efron. He appeared in Sam Mendes's *Away We Go*.

Zach Galifianakis's first stand-up gig was in the back of a hamburger restaurant in Times Square. He now travels the country doing stand-up and appears regularly on late-night talk shows. He lives in Venice Beach, California.

Janeane Garofalo is a comedian, writer, political activist, and retired bike messenger.

Daniel Handler is the author of the novels *The Basic Eight*, *Watch Your Mouth*, and *Adverbs*, and far too many books as Lemony Snicket. He lives in San Francisco with his wife and child.

Todd Hanson is a writer and editor for *The Onion: America's Finest News Source*. He lives in Brooklyn with his two cats, James Boswell and Dr. Samuel Johnson.

Tim Heidecker and **Eric Wareheim** are the costars, writers, and creators of such Cartoon Network shows as *Tom Goes to the Mayor* and *Tim and Eric Awesome Show, Great Job!*

Ed Helms is a former correspondent on *The Daily Show with Jon Stewart*, a cast member of the NBC series *The Office*, and a costar of the hit film *The Hangover*. His upcoming projects include *The Goods* and an as-yet-untitled comedy about Civil War reenactors.

Buck Henry wrote the screenplays for *The Graduate*, *Catch-22*, *The Owl and the Pussycat*, and *To Die For*, among many others. He cocreated and wrote the TV series *Get Smart*, was a writer/performer on *The Steve Allen Show*, *That Was the Week That Was*, and *The New Show*, and hosted *Saturday Night Live* ten times.

Mindy Kaling is a writer, actor, and producer for NBC's *The Office*. She cowrote and costarred in the hit off-Broadway play *Matt & Ben*. She played an object of unwanted affection in both *The 40-Year-Old Virgin* and *Curb Your Enthusiasm*.

Thomas Lennon has starred in *Reno 911!*, *Viva Variety*, and *The State*, among other TV shows and films. He also works as a screenwriter.

Al Madrigal is an extremely funny and underappreciated comedian, actor, writer, and father who resides in Los Angeles in a small home that has lost nearly all of its equity. He can be found performing stand-up comedy tirelessly at low-budget comedy clubs all over the country.

Aasif Mandvi is a correspondent for *The Daily Show with Jon Stewart*. He also wrote and starred in the Obie-winning one-man show *Sakina's Restaurant*. He's appeared in many films, TV shows, and stage plays. If you are interested in knowing more about Aasif Mandvi, please go to Google.com and type his name.

Marc Maron is a stand-up comic, author, actor, radio personality, and Jew. His book, *The Jerusalem Syndrome: My Life as a Reluctant Messiah*, is out of print and overpriced by vendors who think it might have some collector's value.

Adam McKay is a director and writer of movies including *Anchorman* and *Talladega Nights*, and also cofounded the website Funny or Die. He was head writer of *Saturday Night Live* in the late '90s and a cofounder of the Upright Citizens Brigade.

Eugene Mirman's first book, *The Will to Whatevs*, is available now from HarperCollins. Eugene can be seen on HBO's *Flight of the Conchords* and on the new Adult Swim series *Delocated*. He tours regularly and released a new comedy album on Sub Pop in 2009. He has four hundred children and lives in outer space.

Morgan Murphy is a stand-up comedian and writer. She has been on TV and in a movie. On three occasions, she has jogged.

Bob Odenkirk seems capable of anything he sets his mind to, except for summing himself up in thirty words or less.

John Oliver is currently a writer and correspondent for *The Daily Show with Jon Stewart*. He is also a fully qualified subject of the queen. He lives in New York City.

Patton Oswalt is a writer/actor/comedian/producer/asthmatic who lives in Burbank, California.

Martha Plimpton currently makes her living on Broadway, speaking loudly in front of thousands of strangers while pretending they are not there. In the past year she has done two Shakespeare plays and a trilogy by Tom Stoppard, *The Coast of Utopia*, for which she received a Tony Award nomination and a Drama Desk Award.

Harold Ramis is a Chicago-based film director, screenwriter, actor, and producer. His credits include *Animal House*, *Caddyshack*, *Stripes*, *Vacation*, *Ghostbusters*, *Groundhog Day*, *Multiplicity*, *Analyze This*, *Bedazzled*, *The Ice Harvest*, and *Year One*.

Amy Sedaris is an acclaimed career waitress who occasionally writes and performs when her schedule permits. She lives in New York City.

Sarah Silverman is a comedian and actress. She has her own TV show on Comedy Central called *The Sarah Silverman Program*. If you shave the hair away, she has a beautiful face.

Paul F. Tompkins has been performing stand-up comedy for what feels like forever. You can see him on television via *Best Week Ever* and *Countdown with Keith Olbermann*. Mr. Tompkins was born in the 1900s.

Sarah Vowell's books include *Assassination Vacation* and *The Partly Cloudy Patriot*. She is a contributing editor for public radio's *This American Life*.

David Wain is a New York–based director, writer, and actor. You may know him from *Stella* (the megasmash Comedy Central series), *Wet Hot American Summer* (the cult film he directed and cowrote), or *The State* (the critically acclaimed MTV comedy series).

Rainn Wilson is best known for playing Dwight Schrute on the NBC series *The Office.* He's also appeared in movies such as *Almost Famous*, *Juno*, *The Rocker*, and the upcoming *Hesher* and *Peep World.*

Lizz Winstead is cocreator of *The Daily Show with Jon Stewart* and cofounder of Air America Radio. Currently, Lizz stars in *Wake Up World*, an off-Broadway and Web show; tours the country doing stand-up; and is a contributor on MSNBC's *The Ed Show.*